THE RIGHT OF PRIVACY
A Symposium

SYMPOSIA ON LAW AND SOCIETY
GENERAL EDITOR: LEONARD W. LEVY
Claremont Graduate School

THE RIGHT OF PRIVACY

A Symposium on the Implications of
Griswold v. *Connecticut*
381 U.S. 479 (1965)

ROBERT G. DIXON, JR.   PAUL G. KAUPER
THOMAS I. EMERSON   ROBERT B. MCKAY
ARTHUR E. SUTHERLAND

DA CAPO PRESS • NEW YORK • 1971

The papers contained in this volume appeared originally in the *Michigan Law Review,* Volume 64, Number 2 (December 1965), under the title, "Symposium on the *Griswold* Case and the Right of Privacy." They are reprinted by permission of the Editors of the *Michigan Law Review.*

Published by Da Capo Press
A Division of Plenum Publishing Corporation
227 West 17th Street, New York, N.Y. 10011

Manufactured in the United States of America

CONTENTS

THE RIGHT OF PRIVACY
A Symposium

THE *GRISWOLD* PENUMBRA: CONSTITUTIONAL CHARTER FOR AN EXPANDED LAW OF PRIVACY?

Robert G. Dixon, Jr.*

WHEN an "uncommonly silly law"[1] produces the "most significant decision"[2] of the Supreme Court term, and the seven-man majority has to be held together with four opinions, some inquiry is in order. Either there is some hyperbole in the terms "silly" and "significant," or we are witnessing the birth of a new facet of constitutional meaning as an offshoot of a rather special case concerning Connecticut's attempted prohibition of birth control *clinics* through the utilization of its statute prohibiting the *use* of contraceptives.

Griswold v. Connecticut[3] contains the clearest articulation to date (although it is none too clear at that) of the constitutional foundations of a yearning for "privacy," which constitutes a major component of "the American dream." More subjective even than "liberty" and "justice," the "privacy" idea overlaps both, and even turns back on itself to create internal contradictions. For example, privacy is an activist concept supporting freedom of expression in the associational privacy cases. But it is a passivist concept—the right to be let alone—in the school prayer and Bible-reading area, where it has been argued, without explicit judicial recognition as yet,[4] that even an excusal system does not save the regulation, because the necessary requirement of self-identification (in order to obtain permission to absent oneself) itself constitutes an invasion of privacy. Nevertheless, there is a common feature of the two concepts—an interest in nondisclosure of one's identity.

If what follows is as long on privacy in general as on *Griswold*, it is because the case is longer on yearning than on substantive content.

---

* Professor of Law, George Washington University.—Ed.

1. Griswold v. Connecticut, 381 U.S. 479, 527 (1965) (Stewart, J., dissenting).

2. Keeffe, *Practicing Lawyers' Guide to the Current Law Magazines*, 51 A.B.A.J. 885 (1965).

3. 381 U.S. 479 (1965).

4. See School Dist. v. Schempp, 374 U.S. 203, 319 (1963) (Stewart, J., dissenting); Illinois *ex rel.* McCollum v. Board of Educ., 333 U.S. 203, 227 (1948) (Frankfurter, J., concurring).

1

The editors' invitation to discuss the case has prompted a rethinking of a temporarily postponed project on a synthesis on privacy—a task easier to outline than to execute.

All that *Griswold* actually decided was that a statutory system which operated to make it a crime for married couples to use contraceptives (although there was not even a hint of direct enforcement), and for clinics to conduct examinations and prescribe contraceptives (which was the actual enforcement issue), was unconstitutional. The substantive statute merely prohibited contraceptive use; a general aiding and abetting statute furnished the grounds for suppression of the clinic. In order to reach (or create) a privacy issue, the Court allowed the sole defendants—Mrs. Griswold, the clinic director, and Dr. Buxton, the clinic medical director—to assert the rights of married clients of the clinic. The case was discussed judicially, therefore, as though the key issue was state scrutiny of the marital couch; questions concerning the validity of regulations on the manufacture, distribution, and sale of contraceptives, and concerning the validity of the regulation of birth control clinics absent an anti-contraceptive use statute were left unresolved.

To reach the conclusion that the Connecticut laws were unconstitutional, Mr. Justice Douglas, writing the opinion of the Court, first took a broad view of "standing" to assert the rights of third parties, and then, on the merits, ranged broadly through the Bill of Rights, talking loosely about "zones of privacy"[5] directly or peripherally protected by the first, third, fourth, fifth, and ninth amendments. In even broader fashion, Mr. Justice Goldberg took great pains to revive the "forgotten" ninth amendment,[6] so that it emerges especially suited to support whatever "other rights" can be articulated.

The comments that follow are divided into a brief review, for purposes of perspective, of the elusive nature of "privacy" as developed in American law to date, and an attempted rigorous analysis of the privacy aspects of *Griswold*. A final section suggests that effectuation of the new constitutional right of marital privacy necessarily or derivatively implies a corollary right of access to birth control information and devices—a right which should have been more clearly articulated by the Court.

---

5. 381 U.S. at 484.
6. *Id.* at 490 n.6, referring to PATTERSON, THE FORGOTTEN NINTH AMENDMENT (1955).

I. PROLEGOMENON ON PRIVACY

One of the warmest words in the literature of political and legal philosophy is "privacy." Characterized as the "right to be let alone"[7] in Mr. Justice Brandeis' oft-quoted statement, it has been accorded first rank as the most valued right of civilized men. Few concepts, however, are more vague or less amenable to definition and structured treatment than privacy. Under this emotional term march a whole congeries of interests, some closely interrelated, some almost wholly unrelated and even inconsistent. Two broad, variant strands are the "public law" meaning of privacy and the "private law" meaning of privacy, but even within these two broad categories quite different species of claims and conflict arise, and loose terminology abounds.

A. *"Privacy" in Private Law*

In the robust tradition of the common law, as was so well summarized in the seminal essay by Warren and Brandeis on the private-law meaning of privacy,[8] little redress was available for the more refined forms of intrusion by one private person on the solitude and psychic integrity of another. Unless the invasion amounted to a trespass or a nuisance, or could be characterized as a breach of confidence or of implied contract, or affected something like a letter in which the aggrieved party could assert a property interest of sorts, relief was not forthcoming. The major contribution of Warren and Brandeis was in showing through rigorous critical analysis that doctrines of trespass, nuisance, and property were inadequate for the occasion, and that a new concept of protectible privacy could and should be evolved, both as a basis for an intelligible rationale for the handful of existing cases and for future development.

In the process of evolution, what seemed like a single concept has been refined into a loose conglomeration of four torts which, as Dean Prosser has noted,[9] have little in common other than interference with a person's "right to be let alone." The four torts are (1) intrusion on physical solitude or seclusion; (2) publication of unpleasant, although non-defamatory, information about a person; (3) placing of a person in a false but not necessarily defamatory position in the public eye (for example, by attributing to him views that he does

---

7. Olmstead v. United States, 277 U.S. 438, 478 (1928) (Brandeis, J., dissenting).
8. Warren & Brandeis, *The Right to Privacy*, 4 HARV. L. REV. 193 (1890).
9. PROSSER, TORTS 832 (3d ed. 1964).

not hold); (4) unauthorized commercial use of a person's name or picture. From a functional standpoint it appears that two quite different interests are being protected: freedom from physical intrusion on solitude, and freedom from unwanted communication about oneself. Use of the term "right of privacy" as an index heading is confined almost exclusively to these private torts, in addition to some governmental search and seizure matters, wiretapping-eavesdropping, and self-incrimination.

Dean Prosser has appropriately observed that the courts have been so preoccupied with the question whether the tort exists at all that there has been little discussion of its juristic nature and limitations. However, his own suggestion of substituting a generic tort—intentional infliction of mental suffering—hardly seems adequate, because in few of the privacy cases is there "pure" malice. The presence of other interests, which explains such limiting doctrines as the press privilege of dissemination of "newsworthy" information, indicates that a balancing process must be going on, although it is not always clearly articulated what is being balanced, particularly on behalf of the injured party. An "intentional infliction" doctrine could render the right of privacy in tort law overly narrow, in the process of making it more absolute. For this reason there is much appeal in a recent attempt to keep attention focused on privacy as an aspect of human dignity, or, indeed, as a "spiritual interest"[10] rather than merely as an interest in property and reputation. Although such an approach may not make cases any easier to solve, it may help to keep attention focused on those elements of privacy which make it uniquely valued among laymen, who, after all, are the customers of the law.

B. *"Privacy" in Public Law*

In regard to the relations between a government and its citizens, the use of the term "right of privacy" suggests issues and values quite different from those encountered in private law. The term nowhere appears in the Constitution, but is quite obviously a background interest underlying the specific guarantees of the third, fourth, and fifth amendments in regard to quartering of troops, search and seizure, and self-incrimination. Important as the last two categories

---

10. Bloustein, *Privacy as an Aspect of Human Dignity*, 39 N.Y.U.L. REV. 962 (1964). Professor Bloustein's article was prepared under the auspices of the Special Committee on Science and Law of the Association of the Bar of the City of New York, as part of its study examining the impact of modern technology upon privacy.

are, they represent well-established categories already subjected to extensive discussion. Furthermore, although they overlap to a degree the private tort of intrusion upon solitude, neither has been deemed germane to at least two of the several major, recurring "privacy" problems of our time—wiretapping and eavesdropping,[11] and free-wheeling legislative investigations of persons unable or unwilling to plead self-incrimination.[12]

If the fourth and fifth amendments are deemed to exhaust the field of constitutional protection of privacy, then it is a rather narrow field and one unbefitting the concept of privacy as the pre-eminent right of civilized men. However, there are a number of additional outreaches of privacy in American public law, albeit of uncertain dimension, as manifestations of the continuing development of the first amendment and of the concept of due process. Examples include the various privacies associated with the field of religion and belief,[13] privacy in politics, including the secret ballot[14] and nondisclosure of political or social beliefs and associations,[15] the scope of employee duties of candor and disclosure,[16] the use of non-Communist oaths and oaths in general,[17] statutory protection of the solitude of householders by restrictions on canvassing,[18] freedom of associational choice, including self-segregation, in "private" housing, education, and other fields.[19]

Of course, apart from the question of specific constitutional protection of privacy, the American concept of limited government

11. On Lee v. United States, 343 U.S. 747 (1952); Olmstead v. United States, 277 U.S. 438 (1928); *cf.* Silverman v. United States, 365 U.S. 505 (1961).

12. Wilkinson v. United States, 365 U.S. 399 (1961); Braden v. United States, 365 U.S. 431 (1961); Barenblatt v. United States, 360 U.S. 109 (1959); *cf.* Deutch v. United States, 367 U.S. 456 (1961).

13. It is questionable whether privacy is furthered by West Virginia State Bd. of Educ. v. Barnette, 319 U.S. 624 (1943), which granted a broad exemption from a flag salute requirement in the interest of a general freedom of speech and belief, but allowed the flag salute requirement to continue. See Dixon, *Religion, Schools, and the Open Society: A Socio-Constitutional Issue,* 13 J. Pub. L. 267, 281-88 (1965).

14. Nutting, *Freedom of Silence—Constitutional Protection Against Governmental Intrusions in Political Affairs,* 47 Mich. L. Rev. 181 (1948).

15. Gibson v. Florida Legislative Investigation Comm., 372 U.S. 539 (1963); NAACP v. Alabama *ex rel.* Patterson, 357 U.S. 449 (1958).

16. Beilan v. Board of Pub. Educ., 357 U.S. 399 (1958); Lerner v. Casey, 357 U.S. 468 (1958); Slochower v. Board of Higher Educ., 350 U.S. 551 (1956).

17. Baggett v. Bullitt, 377 U.S. 360 (1964); Cramp v. Board of Pub. Instruction, 368 U.S. 278 (1961); Torcaso v. Watkins, 367 U.S. 488 (1961); Wieman v. Updegraff, 344 U.S. 183 (1952).

18. Breard v. Alexandria, 341 U.S. 622 (1951).

19. Avins, *The Right Not To Listen,* 51 A.B.A.J. 656 (1965); Avins, *Freedom of Choice in Personal Service Occupations—Thirteenth Amendment Limitations on Anti-discrimination Legislation,* 49 Cornell L.Q. 228 (1964); Avins, *Prima Facie Tort and Injunction—New Remedies Against Sitdowns,* 24 Ga. B.J. 20 (1961).

formerly helped to maximize privacy by affording a protection of sorts to economic, social, and racial *laissez-faire.* This domain of privacy inherent in a system of limited government has now been considerably eroded by the freeing of federal legislative power through broad construction of the commerce and expenditure clauses, and by the demise of substantive due process as a check on economic and social legislation.[20] Both the purpose and the effect of the new legislative norms and extensive administrative regulation are to diminish the area of "free" contract, a supposed freedom resting at times on imbalances in knowledge and bargaining power between investor and dealer, worker and employer, and supplier and manufacturer. But the impact of much of the regulation may not be so much to diminish the right to be let alone as to diminish a power to act as one pleases without regard to external impacts, which is not quite the same thing.

C. *The Idea of Privacy*

A lengthy essay could be written on the historical evolution of privacy concepts[21] from the early Greek "politics of participation," in which personal virtue was equated with civic virtue and privacy had no place, to the robust individualism of the American frontier, where the mores of society forbade inquiry into a man's past. Suffice it to say that the exploration would entail inquiry into the Judeo-Christian concept of the "soul," that recessive, untouchable essence of man, the Germanic concept of the "folk," in which the individual found his true identity and expression, and the Reformation theory of direct and personal relation to God. In a study of the modern era, particular stress would have to be placed on the natural-rights movement, which postulates the intrinsic value of pre-social personal status and absolute birthrights; on the abstrusities of Rousseau, where the absorption of the individual will into the socialized "general will" implies total abnegation of privacy; and on the recent pragmatic evolution of democratic socialism and the security state, in which the forces of organization threaten to crowd out privacy and, indeed, all of the passive virtues.[22]

---

20. McCloskey, *Economic Due Process and the Supreme Court*, 1962 SUP. CT. REV. 34.

21. See generally SABINE, A HISTORY OF POLITICAL THEORY (rev. ed. 1950).

22. The growing corporate and government practice of psychiatric evaluation and psychological testing of employees poses interesting questions about the range and depth of probing, about the limits of required disclosure to employers, and about means of safeguarding against arbitrariness in the use of such data by employers.

The extent to which one finds privacy interests and threatened invasions of privacy interests depends largely on how the term is defined, or, if definition is impossible, how the term is conceived. Many commentators[23] have begun with the broad and warm Brandeisian invocation of a "right to be let alone." But only a hermit living outside society has such a right; unqualified, the "right" flies in the face of all social control. For what purpose is a person let alone? Are social purposes served by the right so that, in according recognition to the right, society is actually serving its long-term interest while restraining its immediate impulse to assert control? Does society, by recognizing the right, preserve and encourage personal well-springs of creativity and differentiation—needed by society if it is to avoid stagnation—which would be stifled by compelled conformity to majoritarian values and practices? Or is a "social" justification of privacy a self-defeating thing, undercutting the essence of the privacy interest? Is being let alone an end in itself as part of the dignity of man, akin to a natural right, needing no utilitarian justification in terms of social product? In short, is privacy *intrinsic* or *derivative*?

Obviously, radically different approaches originate in these different premises. Even though it be granted that a balancing of competing claims, values, and "goods" is always present as part of the never-ending process of reasoned choice, it still may make a world of difference whether one postulates social control and demands that privacy prove its social utility, or postulates privacy and counsels official restraint even where the privacy "good" is uncertain and the official action is aimed toward a "good" end. The latter approach is not quite the same thing as the "preferred position" approach in regard to freedom of expression, because in evaluating freedoms of expression we are weighing an identifiable, outward-looking course of conduct against competing social standards and interests. Speech, publication, and parades involve overt measurable *conduct* rather than privacy. It is only when we turn to a freedom of non-expression or inaction that privacy as a distinctive concept enters the calculus.

Freedoms of expression can exist without enjoying a "preferred" position, although their exact content may be affected. But to deny to privacy the character of a self-justifying end is, perforce, to socialize it; and to socialize it is to foredoom it to unequal competition with easily perceived, immediate, and pressing needs of society.[24]

---

23. *E.g.*, Griswold, *The Right To Be Let Alone*, 55 Nw. U.L. Rev. 216 (1960).
24. "Once privacy is invaded, privacy is gone." Public Util. Comm'n v. Pollak, 343 U.S. 451, 469 (1952) (Douglas, J., dissenting).

The free-speech claimant asserts deviant views and values; the privacy claimant doesn't want to play ball at all. The former is still part of the open society and fights his battle in the marketplace of ideas; the latter is part of the closed society and fights to withhold his allegiance and perhaps even his identity and associations.

The premise of intrinsic privacy as an end in itself is clearly perceived in the fourth amendment, where we start with the nearly absolute premise that a man's home is his castle, and the fifth amendment, where we accord silence and secrecy to the known or putative criminal.[25] Outside these areas, life situations may blur the distinctions between *intrinsic* privacy and socially *derivative* privacy, and the quite continuous blurring in judicial usage has made a reasoned evolution of a distinctive privacy concept quite difficult, if not impossible. For example, is associational privacy, which the NAACP has recently achieved but the Communist Party has not,[26] an independent right, protecting a basic secrecy-solitude interest? Or is it a derivative benefit, supporting freedom of political action and having no independent significance? If it is the latter, should not some term other than "associational privacy" be used, such as "freedom of secret association for public action"?

A further problem in the prevalent loose characterizations of privacy as the "right to be let alone" is that the right tends to become indistinguishable from a policy of *laissez-faire*, promoting general freedom of action. One possibility for separating "privacy" from "freedom" as juristic concepts would be to focus on the idea of limits upon society's power either to *make exposure* or *force disclosure* of matters which the individual would prefer to keep secret. Thus narrowed, the term would be removed from the area of general *laissez-faire* interest, but the privacy concept might then be too narrow, because it would be revealed as centering really on an interest in "secrecy," which is not a "warm" idea at all. Even though we have achieved the secret ballot in order to ensure an exact translation of private views into public choice, the "stand up and be counted" slogan still has wide appeal as indicative of a robust and

25. Barrett, *Personal Rights, Property Rights, and the Fourth Amendment,* 1960 SUP. CT. REV. 46.

26. *Compare* Gibson v. Florida Legislative Investigation Comm., 372 U.S. 539 (1963), *with* Barenblatt v. United States, 360 U.S. 109 (1959). While this article was in galley the Supreme Court, on grounds of self-incrimination, set aside orders under the Subversive Activities Control Act of 1950 compelling registration of Communist Party members. Albertson v. Subversive Activities Control Bd., 86 Sup. Ct. 194 (1965).

fearless honesty. Secrecy commonly conveys a connotation of forbidden conspiracies, and conspiracies find few defenders.[27]

Secrecy nevertheless may be an important component of the core idea of privacy as a public-law concept, and to this probably should be added the factor of "solitude"—freedom from certain social impositions and pressures. The meaning of privacy, as thus refined and separated from a generalized concept of freedom, may be fairly well encompassed by the twin ideas of *secrecy*, which protects the nondisclosure interest, and *solitude*, which protects against coercions of belief or, derivatively, against actions designed to make the holding of belief uncomfortable, or against any undue social intrusions on the intimacies and dignities of life. As already noted, however, these twin ideas are Janus-faced, because secrecy in the context of associational privacy is an *activist* concept supporting political action, whereas solitude in the context of nondisclosure of nonconformity is a *passivist*, right-to-be-let-alone concept.

When marital privacy is recognized, and then used to defend birth control clinics, an added dimension, which is neither secrecy nor solitude, seems to appear—a right of access to information relevant to the specific condition of privacy at issue. To this we now turn.

II. *Griswold* AND THE RIGHT TO PRIVACY

What does *Griswold* add to the judicial literature on the dimensions of privacy in its constitutional or public-law aspects? It does little, certainly, to clarify the conceptual dimensions of the privacy concept. But it does much to provide varied and flexible constitutional underpinnings for those situations which do not fit established categories neatly but still seem to rest on values thought to be vital and which, for lack of a better term, are called privacy. In *Griswold* the Court avoided defining privacy narrowly and particularly, and also avoided tying it to one or two supporting (but also necessarily limiting) clauses in the Constitution. By the very breadth and uncertainty of the opinions, especially the opinion of Mr. Justice Douglas for the Court—an opinion which roams through the Bill of Rights picking up a letter here and another there to spell out the new

---

27. See, *e.g.*, Dennis v. United States, 341 U.S. 494, 577 (1951) (Jackson, J., concurring): "The law of conspiracy has been the chief means at the Government's disposal to deal with the growing problems created by such organizations. I happen to think it is an awkward and inept remedy, but I find no constitutional authority for taking this weapon from the Government. There is no constitutional right to 'gang up' on the Government."

right—the door was left open for continued probing and refinement of the privacy principle.

A. *The Penumbral Approach*

There is already a rich terrain to be investigated and a great need for closer analysis, as indicated by the varied content of the "zones of privacy,"[28] and by the range of controversy over "penumbral rights of 'privacy and repose,' "[29] suggested by the cases cited by Mr. Justice Douglas, who mentioned more than a half dozen "privacy" situations. For example, the new derivative first amendment right of associational privacy was articulated in *NAACP v. Alabama ex rel. Patterson*[30] as the "freedom to associate and privacy in one's associations." The right of religious belief was supported by *West Virginia State Board of Educ. v. Barnette.*[31] The right to be undisturbed by the doorbell ringing of commercial solicitors was supported in *Breard v. Alexandria.*[32] The right to be undisturbed by music and spoken advertisements while riding in public conveyances was denied by a sharply divided Court in *Public Utilities Comm'n v. Pollak.*[33] The right to be free from unreasonable search and seizure received added protection through the extension to the state courts of the exclusionary rule regarding illegally seized evidence in *Mapp v. Ohio,*[34] and was further strengthened in *Monroe v. Pape,*[35] which dealt with the liability under the federal constitution of municipal police officers for illegal invasion and search of a home. The privacy of the jail cell was viewed dimly, but apparently not completely eradicated, in the recent dispute in *Lanza v. New York*[36] over the use of evidence obtained by eavesdropping. The sanctity of the household, at least a household graced by a half-ton pile of trash and rodent feces, had to give way to permit rat-control inspection without a warrant—but only by a 5-4 vote.[37] Mr. Justice Douglas also alluded in *Griswold* to *Skinner v. Oklahoma ex rel. Williamson,*[38] which invalidated Oklahoma's provision for compulsory sterilization of certain categories of habitual criminals, although his own opinion

---

28. 381 U.S. at 484.
29. *Id.* at 485.
30. 357 U.S. 449, 462 (1958).
31. 319 U.S. 624 (1943).
32. 341 U.S. 622 (1951).
33. 343 U.S. 451 (1952).
34. 367 U.S. 643 (1961).
35. 365 U.S. 167 (1961).
36. 370 U.S. 139 (1962).
37. Frank v. Maryland, 359 U.S. 360 (1959).
38. 316 U.S. 535 (1942).

for the Court in *Skinner* had stood not on the ground of intrinsic privacies in procreation, but rather on the denial of equal protection involved in the classification scheme used in the statute.

The foregoing cases were simply listed by Mr. Justice Douglas and were not subjected to a fresh conceptual discussion; there was no attempt either to interrelate them or to use their particularity as a way of getting at a possible general central value of privacy. The list certainly reveals, however, a rich potpourri of privacy matters, and more certainly could be added; Mr. Justice Douglas was only using illustrative examples with no intention of being exhaustive.

B. *The "Forgotten" Ninth Amendment*

The concurring opinion of Mr. Justice Goldberg, joined by the Chief Justice and Mr. Justice Brennan, rests on the ninth amendment, and, indeed, constitutes the first major judicial treatment of the ninth amendment, which states: "The enumeration in the Constitution, of certain rights, shall not be construed to deny or disparage others retained by the people."

Mr. Justice Goldberg's focus on the ninth amendment does not narrow the breadth and multiplicity of the zones of privacy suggested by Mr. Justice Douglas. His special stress on the almost unfathomable ninth amendment strongly reaffirms the preëxisting constitutional tradition of using substantive due process as a broad vehicle for judicial articulation and protection of "fundamental liberties," whether or not they are specified elsewhere in the Constitution. And the ultimate effect may be to heighten the prospects for judicial support, case by case, for a broader range of "privacy" situations and of other hard-to-classify interests which, despite their vagueness, should be "retained by the people" in a democratic public order strongly committed to preserving individuality.

There may very well be some past denials of privacy claims, such as those involved with the music and advertising programs in public conveyances that were at issue in *Pollak*, which might strike the Court differently if passed in review again under the ninth amendment. Tactically, of course, use of the ninth amendment could be a basis for reaching a contrary result without the necessity of reversing the earlier decisions. Mr. Justice Goldberg's approach, in short, does not offer assistance in defining privacy, but is at least congenial to further probing and experimentation.

C. *Substantive Due Process and Privacy*

The separate concurrences of Mr. Justice Harlan and of Mr. Justice White, although related more to general principles of constitutional interpretation and statutory analysis than to privacy *per se*, are not uncongenial to continued attempts to develop privacy as a more general constitutional principle than heretofore. Earlier, in the unsuccessful *Poe v. Ullman*[39] challenge to the same Connecticut statute, Mr. Justice Harlan had made an exceptionally apt statement, which Mr. Justice Goldberg quoted approvingly in *Griswold:*

> Certainly the safeguarding of the home does not follow merely from the sanctity of property rights. The home derives its preeminence as the seat of family life. And the integrity of that life is something so fundamental that it has been found to draw to its protection the principles of more than one explicitly granted Constitutional right. . . . Of this whole "private realm of family life" it is difficult to imagine what is more private or more intimate than a husband and wife's marital relations.[40]

The main thrust of Mr. Justice Harlan's concurring opinion in *Griswold* was to oppose Mr. Justice Black's view that the fourteenth amendment is grounded in the Bill of Rights and impliedly limited thereby.[41] Mr. Justice Harlan would preserve the fourteenth amendment as a perpetually fresh basis for safeguarding basic values "implicit in the concept of ordered liberty."[42]

Mr. Justice White's opinion begins with an acceptance of the Harlan view of the fourteenth amendment and perhaps even enlarges on it. He suggested that a statute with effects like that of the Connecticut statute "bears a substantial burden of justification when attacked under the Fourteenth Amendment,"[43] and then proceeded to an analysis demonstrating that the Connecticut statute was not reasonably related, in its terms and operation, to the legitimate objective of barring extramarital affairs.

D. *Negative View: Privacy and "Clear Meaning"*

Both Mr. Justice Black and Mr. Justice Stewart emerged as dissenters in *Griswold,* but not necessarily as "anti-privatarians." Mr.

---

39. 367 U.S. 497 (1961).
40. 381 U.S. at 495 (concurring opinion) (quoting from Poe v. Ullman, 367 U.S. 497, 551-52 (1961) (Harlan, J., dissenting)).
41. Morrison, *Does the Fourteenth Amendment Incorporate the Bill of Rights?— The Judicial Interpretation,* 2 STAN. L. REV. 140 (1949).
42. Palko v. Connecticut, 302 U.S. 319, 325 (1937).
43. 381 U.S. at 503 (concurring opinion).

Justice Black was the only Justice to stress sufficiently the fact that
" 'privacy' is a broad, abstract and ambiguous concept."[44] Privacy
is broader than any one amendment because several of the specific
guarantees are designed in part to protect something that might be
called privacy, but each guarantee is also broader than privacy.

For example, Mr. Justice Black correctly criticized the tendency
to talk about the fourth amendment "as though it protects nothing
but 'privacy.' "[45] As he pointed out, a person may be more annoyed
by an unceremonious public arrest and consequent search by a policeman than by a seizure in the privacy of his home. Similarly, there
may be something instructive in the common over-use of the "privacy" label by persons writing about the fourth and fifth amendments.[46] Although conceptual clarity is not advanced by the practice,
the writer obtains a title which attracts more interest than would a
"search and seizure" label, and which evokes an instinctively sym-
pathetic emotional response. This observation applies equally to
the over-use of the privacy label by writers in the field of libel and
slander, or on tort-law protections of other aspects of personality.[47]

The main thrust of Mr. Justice Black's dissent, however, lies
elsewhere. While he likes his privacy "as well as the next one,"[48] he
recognizes a right of the government to invade it, not when there is
a counterbalancing governmental interest (heresy!), but whenever
government is not "prohibited by some specific constitutional provision."[49] The remainder of the dissent develops further his theories
of constitutional interpretation. It may come as a surprise to some
to find that all Mr. Justice Black has been doing in his constitutional
adjudication, at least in his own self-analysis, is to apply the "clear
meaning" of the constitutional text.[50] Be that as it may, his "clear

44. *Id.* at 509 (dissenting opinion).
45. *Ibid.*
46. See, *e.g.*, Beaney, *The Constitutional Right to Privacy in the Supreme Court*, 1962 Sup. Ct. Rev. 212. Compare King, *Electronic Surveillance and Constitutional Rights*, 33 Geo. Wash. L. Rev. 240 (1964), an essay with a modest title but with a sensitive perception of larger privacy issues and the need for a penumbral approach in constitutional interpretation in this field.
47. See Ernst & Schwartz, Privacy—The Right To Be Let Alone (1962); Hofstadter & Horowitz, The Right of Privacy (1964); Bloustein, *supra* note 10.
48. 381 U.S. at 510 (dissenting opinion).
49. *Ibid.*
50. See Mendelson, Justices Black and Frankfurter—Conflict in the Court 51-60 (1961); Frantz, *The First Amendment in the Balance*, 71 Yale L.J. 1424 (1962); Mendelson, *On the Meaning of the First Amendment—Absolutes in the Balance*, 50 Calif. L. Rev. 821 (1962); Frantz, *Is the First Amendment Law?—A Reply to Professor Mendelson*, 51 Calif. L. Rev. 729 (1963); Mendelson, *The First Amendment and the Judicial Process—A Reply to Mr. Frantz*, 17 Vand. L. Rev. 479 (1964). See also Black

meaning" yielded no protection for privacy in this instance. It may
not be too clear to some students of constitutional law why, under
Mr. Justice Black's "clear meaning" analysis, obscenity,[51] group
libel,[52] and associational privacy[53] are constitutional absolutes along
with simple free speech, while marital privacy, in the *Griswold* context of access to birth control information, is no part of the due-
process liberty which the fourteenth amendment applies to the states.
And is it just the "clear meaning" of the fourteenth amendment
which requires a nationally uniform practice in regard to exclusion
of illegally seized evidence,[54] standards of self-incrimination and
immunity statutes,[55] and the right to counsel?[56] To pursue these
questions, which are essentially questions of methods of constitutional interpretation, would take us away from the subject of privacy
and should be handled in a separate paper.

Although Mr. Justice Black's "clear meaning" did not in this
instance yield a privacy shield for Mrs. Griswold or contraceptives
for her clients, there is always the possibility that the "clear meaning" of the Constitution may yield privacy protection in other fact
situations. One aspect of "clear meaning" jurisprudence is its un-
predictability, in the guise of being best articulated.[57] It can be

& Cahn, *Justice Black and First Amendment "Absolutes"—A Public Interview*, 37
N.Y.U.L. Rev. 549 (1962).

51. Roth v. United States, 354 U.S. 476, 514 (1957) (Black & Douglas, JJ., dissenting).
52. Beauharnais v. Illinois, 343 U.S. 250, 275 (1952) (Black, J., dissenting).
53. Gibson v. Florida Legislative Investigation Comm., 372 U.S. 539, 559 (1963)
(Black, J., concurring).
54. Mapp v. Ohio, 367 U.S. 643, 661 (1961) (Black, J., concurring).
55. Malloy v. Hogan, 378 U.S. 1 (1964), Mr. Justice Black voted with the majority.
56. Gideon v. Wainwright, 372 U.S. 335 (1963).
57. That "clear meaning" may not leave clear tracks and ensure predictability is
indicated by the surprise some liberals felt in regard to Mr. Justice Black's recent
support of state power in the 1964 sit-in decisions (see especially his dissenting opinions in Bell v. Maryland, 378 U.S. 226, 318 (1964), and Bouie v. City of Columbia, 378
U.S. 347, 363 (1964)), his dissent in Cox v. Louisiana, 379 U.S. 559, 575 (1965), from
the Court's reversal of convictions for picketing near the courthouse, and his dissent
in *Griswold* itself. In *Cox* he said: "Those who encourage minority groups to believe
that the United States Constitution and federal laws give them a right to patrol and
picket in the streets whenever they choose, in order to advance what they think to
be a just and noble end, do no service to those minority groups, their cause, or their
country." 379 U.S. at 584. If picketing is a form of free speech, Thornhill v. Alabama,
310 U.S. 88 (1940), this language, whether sound or unsound, is something less than
first amendment absolutism.
See also Hannah v. Larche, 363 U.S. 420 (1960), where, with civil rights and civil
liberties interests in conflict, Justices Douglas and Black in dissent would have barred
the Civil Rights Commission from using confidential informants and from forbidding
cross-examination in its hearings on alleged violations by the state of Louisiana of
Negro rights. Was it only the "clear meaning" theory that kept Justices Douglas and
Black in dissent, while the other half of the liberal block, the Chief Justice and Mr.
Justice Brennan, split off and supported the Commission?

viewed as really a *code* jurisprudence rather than a *common-law* jurisprudence, although this may involve re-assessing Mr. Justice Black as a frustrated Napoleonic jurist. Perhaps its prime virtue is that it can lead to a quick "up-dating" of constitutional meaning without the need to worry much about the baggage of precedent. And its lack of "balancing" makes a "Brandeis brief" approach irrelevant. It lies, in short, at the opposite pole from that much-maligned and usually totally misunderstood term, "neutral principles."[58]

E. *Negative View: Is the Issue Privacy, or Access to Information?*

Although Justices Black and Stewart joined in each others' dissents, the opinion written by Mr. Justice Stewart was quite unlike that written by Mr. Justice Black. It was Stewart who coined the phrase "uncommonly silly law,"[59] a characterization of the statute which caught the fancy of the press and appeared in numerous editorials. By "silly," he seems to have meant that the law was "obviously unenforceable, except in the oblique context of the present case."[60]

Although he did not pursue the point, this thought may have been an oblique attack by Mr. Justice Stewart on the issue of standing. Mr. Justice Douglas' opinion for the Court was the only opinion to discuss the problem of standing, which had defeated earlier attacks on the statute in the *Tileston*[61] and *Poe* cases. In *Griswold*, of course, there had been an actual arrest of birth control clinic operators, whereas *Tileston* and *Poe* were only declaratory-judgment actions by physicians and patients in a setting of recent nonenforcement of the statute. Despite these distinctions, the Court's very brief treatment of standing in *Griswold* is mystifying unless one realizes that the matter had been carefully canvassed in *Poe* just four years earlier, that the vote then was 5-4, and that Mr. Justice Frankfurter, who had written the opinion for the Court in *Poe*, was no longer on the bench.

Nevertheless, there is still the question (and this also may have troubled Mr. Justice Stewart) of how the *Griswold* case became a

---

58. See Stone, *"Result-Orientation" and Appellate Judgment,* in PERSPECTIVES OF LAW: ESSAYS FOR AUSTIN WAKEMAN SCOTT 347 (1964), and the list of "neutral principles" articles therein; Wechsler, *Toward Neutral Principles of Constitutional Law,* 73 HARV. L. REV. 1 (1959).

59. 381 U.S. at 527 (dissenting opinion).

60. *Ibid.*

61. Tileston v. Ullman, 318 U.S. 44 (1943).

right-of-marital-privacy case instead of a birth control clinic-regulatory policy case. It is instructive to remember Mr. Justice Brennan's statement in *Poe* that the true controversy was over the opening of birth control clinics on a large scale. Because he felt that the issue was not presented properly, he concurred in the dismissal of the *Poe* case. Starting with this premise, it would seem that when the birth control clinic issue was raised squarely in *Griswold* by the actual arrest of clinic operators, the Court's discussion should have focused to some extent on the question of the means and ends of state power to regulate birth control clinics. Instead, the dispensers of birth control advice were granted shelter under the marital privacy of users of contraceptives.

To appreciate this aspect of the case it is important to recognize that "standing" in this sequence of birth control cases is at least a two-faceted issue. One facet is the actual threat of harm—the question of the prospect of enforcement on which Mr. Justice Frankfurter's opinion in *Poe* turned. An actual arrest solved this difficulty in *Griswold*. The other facet is the *jus tertii* issue—the standing of the defendant clinic operators to defend themselves by raising the rights of their clients to obtain birth control advice and to act on that advice by using the prescribed contraceptives. In according the defendants standing to raise the constitutional rights of their married clients, Mr. Justice Douglas said simply: "The rights of husband and wife, pressed here, are likely to be diluted or adversely affected unless those rights are considered in a suit involving those who have this kind of confidential relation to them."[62]

Clearly, the "rights of husband and wife" which Mr. Justice Douglas had in mind did not consist merely of an interest in having the statute nullified so that the couple could use contraceptives without fear of police invasion of their bedroom. The interest would have to be the broader one of an *affirmative right of access* to birth control information so that they could regulate, more safely and satisfactorily, the intimacies of their marital relationship.

It was this broad approach toward standing, allowing the defendant clinic to raise the rights of married couples not before the Court, which brought the marital-privacy issue to the fore. This approach also submerged both the more general question of state power to regulate birth control clinics, and Mr. Justice White's concern whether the means chosen were reasonably related to an assumed

---

62. 381 U.S. at 481.

purpose of discouraging sexual promiscuity. The privacy issue thus raised is seen on close analysis not to be simply a right to be let alone; rather, it takes on the aspect of an affirmative right of access to information concerning a very private sphere of life.

It may well be that Mr. Justice Stewart had an additional difficulty with the majority's approach. His robust realism[63] led him to reject the broad language in the majority opinions about preserving the inviolability of the marital chamber, because there was never any real prospect of statutory enforcement in that direction. Granting the clinic defendants standing to raise the issue of a right of marital privacy in the *use* of contraceptives, and handling the case primarily on this basis, does not help their cause from the Stewart perspective; it hurts their cause because it directs attention to an unreal situation and blunts the real issue, which is access to information—and freedom to dispense information—about marital privacies.

Since information relevant to marital privacies is what *Griswold*, functionally viewed, comes down to, it is a pity that the majority and the dissents did not join issue on what might be characterized as a dissemination-of-information and making-privacy-effective type of issue, supported by the first amendment. Both Justices Black and Stewart noted this approach, but brushed it aside, albeit not very convincingly. The approach involves an analysis of the standing and substantive rights of dispensers of birth control information, as well as the standing and substantive rights of recipients of birth control information.

III. EFFECTUATING MARITAL PRIVACY: THE RIGHT OF ACCESS TO BIRTH CONTROL INFORMATION

Merely to phrase the above caption may be to suggest the kind of conceptual confusion which seems to be inherent in the privacy

---

63. See, *e.g.*, his opinions in the reapportionment decisions, Reynolds v. Sims, 377 U.S. 533, 588 (1964), and companion cases in 377 U.S. at 676, 693, 712, and especially 744. Although in the opinion of the present writer (*Reapportionment in the Supreme Court and Congress—Constitutional Struggle for Fair Representation*, 63 MICH. L. REV. 209 (1964)), no Justice covered himself with glory in the *opinions* written in the reapportionment decisions, as distinguished from the *results*, Mr. Justice Stewart came closer than any other to hitting the mark and realizing that the battle concerned representation and not mathematical abstractions about equal masses of census statistics. Also indicative of his realistic approach was his desire for more facts on the actual impact on the child of prayer and Bible-reading practices in public schools before reaching and resolving the constitutional issues. School Dist. v. Schempp, 374 U.S. 203, 319-20 (1963) (dissenting opinion).

field. If privacy is essentially a state of peace and repose which we seek to protect from invasion, does it not take some mental gymnastics to say that *derived* from this premise of privacy, or *associated* with it as part of the core concept, there is a right of access to information relevant to rational use and enjoyment of the state of privacy? But are not both elements unavoidably present in the *Griswold* case, and does not the approach of the Court gloss over the conceptual difficulties? Without the birth control clinic operation, there would have been no case. The only interest of a married couple vis-à-vis the clinic is an interest in obtaining information relevant to a very private part of their lives. By invoking the married couples' fictional fear of prosecution for *use* of contraceptives to give the clinic defendants standing to defend themselves from actual prosecution for giving *advice*, the Court tied marital privacy and access to information together into a single bundle of rights. The Court's approach to standing also in effect reconstituted the facts and issues at the appellate level. Had the reconstituted facts been the actual facts, the decision probably would have been unanimous. To talk of allowing "the police to search the sacred precincts of marital bedrooms for telltale signs of the use of contraceptives"[64] is obviously "repulsive to the notions of privacy surrounding the marriage relationship."[65]

But what about the actual case of clinic operation, and the actual question of the allowable range of that operation? What about the Black-Stewart distinction between mere *advice* and the actual *dissemination* of contraceptives as part of a "planned course of conduct"? If only advice had been involved, Justices Black and Stewart apparently would have joined the majority on free-speech grounds, but with no conscious overlay of marital privacy.

In effect, therefore, the Court used standing as a ploy to avoid discussing these questions, which shape the real issue in the case, and which the caption at the beginning of this section seeks to articulate. The result reached by the Court is clear. The clinic can continue to operate, and married couples, at least, have access to birth control information by resort to the clinic. If this decision rests on the peculiar wording of the Connecticut statute, which proscribed "use," then the decision is very narrow. Repeal of the "use" statute and substitution of a statute regulating or proscribing clinic operation

64. 381 U.S. at 485.
65. *Id.* at 486.

per se would present a fresh situation.[66] But if the Court's stress on "marital privacy" in the use of contraceptives extends to a right of access to birth control information, then the case yields a broad precedent indeed. In rationalizing it, scholars might dispute whether the precedent can be derived from the first amendment alone, or whether the "penumbral" right of privacy is a necessary adjunct.

A perusal of the briefs[67] filed in the Supreme Court in *Griswold* indicates that the attorneys conceived the essence of the appeal to be either a due-process test of whether the Connecticut law was a reasonable means to achieve a proper legislative purpose, or a first amendment test of whether the statute violated any free-speech rights of the acting director of the clinic, Mrs. Griswold, and the medical director, Dr. Buxton. Privacy was handled only in the fictional context of bedroom invasion, with citations to *Rochin v. California*.[68] There was no clear attempt either to extend the assertion of freedom of speech to include the right of clinic patients to obtain birth control information, or to extend the assertion of the right of marital privacy to include a right of access to information intimately related to, and supportive of, conjugal privacy.

Free speech, discussed alone and unrelated to privacy, was phrased variously in the briefs as a right to intellectual freedom,[69] freedom of expression,[70] a right to disseminate information,[71] a right to practice medicine in accord with accepted scientific principles[72] (better phrased perhaps as a right to speak the truth), a right of physicians to advise patients,[73] and a physician's freedom of professional conscience.[74] For Justices Black and Stewart, all of this con-

---

66. It is doubtful, however, that the outcome would be different. The following comment of Mr. Justice White, the only Justice to discuss the actual question of clinic operation, is directly in point: "[T]he clear effect of these statutes, as enforced, is to deny disadvantaged citizens of Connecticut, those without either adequate knowledge or resources to obtain private counseling, access to medical assistance and up-to-date information in respect to proper methods of birth control. . . . In my view, a statute with these effects bears a substantial burden of justification when attacked under the Fourteenth Amendment." 381 U.S. at 503 (concurring opinion).

67. Jurisdictional Statement for Appellants; Motion To Dismiss Appeal for Appellee; Brief for Appellants; Brief for Appellee; Brief for Catholic Council on Civil Liberties as Amicus Curiae; Brief for the American Civil Liberties Union and the Connecticut Civil Liberties Union as Amici Curiae; Brief for Physicians as Amici Curiae.

68. 342 U.S. 165 (1952).

69. Brief for Appellant, p. 17.

70. *Id.* at 20.

71. *Id.* at 23.

72. *Id.* at 67.

73. Jurisdictional Statement for Appellants, p. 6.

74. Brief for Physicians as Amici Curiae.

certed effort focused on a basic free speech-first amendment claim
went down the drain because, as the state had asserted, the "speech"
was too intermixed with a sequence of "action," consisting of physical
examinations, prescriptions, and in some cases the dispensing of birth
control devices, with a graduated scale of fees for those who could
pay.[75] Regarding the merits of the free speech issue per se, one may
note that the "speech"-"action" dichotomy is easier to state than to
apply neatly and consistently, and may contrast Mr. Justice Black
in *Griswold* with Mr. Justice Black in *Dennis v. United States*.[76]
Although Mr. Justice Black objected to the "planned course of conduct" in *Griswold*, it was just this concept that led the majority in
Dennis to affirm the convictions over Mr. Justice Black's dissent.

More relevant to the present discussion, however, is this question:
What would have been the effect of an attempted link-up between
a claim of marital privacy, defined to include a need for information
of the birth control type, and a first amendment claim defined to
include a right against state denial of access to information which is
available and needed for intelligent decision? Such a combination
would not only have closed a logical gap in the case, but would also
have made it more difficult for Justices Black and Stewart to brush
aside the free-speech claim simply on the ground that "action" was
involved. With such a combination, the "action" at issue, which for
Justices Black and Stewart qualified out of existence the first amendment claim of the clinic staff, would appear in a new light as something supportive of the first amendment-information claim of those
who turned to the clinic for help. There would still be a planned
course of conduct, but it would be responsive to a first amendment-
privacy claim of married couples, and the fact the aid went beyond
advice to include the objects described in the advice would seem to
be incidental. When it is sometimes said that speech is an end in itself, what is really denoted is a feeling of the primacy of free speech
as a constitutional value, not that it is a passive entity in an action-
less vacuum.

---

75. After noting that the clinic activity included supplying contraceptive devices,
Mr. Justice Black said: "Thus these defendants admittedly engaged with others in a
planned course of conduct to help people violate the Connecticut law. . . . What
would be the constitutional fate of the law if hereafter applied to punish nothing but
speech is, as I have said, quite another matter." 381 U.S. at 508 (dissenting opinion).
Similarly, Mr. Justice Stewart said: "If all the appellants had done was to advise people that they thought the use of contraceptives was desirable, or even to counsel their
use, the appellants would, of course, have a substantial First Amendment claim. But
their activities went far beyond mere advocacy." *Id.* at 529 n.2 (dissenting opinion).
76. 341 U.S. 494, 579 (1951) (dissenting opinion).

In other words, is not the first amendment claim weak when looked at only from the viewpoint of the dispensing of information, because of the additional "action" factors on the part of the clinic, and far stronger when looked at from the viewpoint of the recipient, especially when it is intermixed with a "making privacy effective" argument? Viewed thus, a finding of "action" should not end the first amendment discussion, but should instead invite further inquiry as to purposes and effects.

IV. CONCLUSION

Elaboration of this suggested theory of an affirmative right of access to birth control information must await further litigation. It might be founded jointly on the first amendment and on the new constitutionally recognized "penumbral" right of marital privacy. Additional support might be forthcoming from the once forgotten but now remembered ninth amendment. If birth control information is available but for the intervening hand of the state, can that hand perhaps be brushed aside by articulating a constitutionally protected ninth amendment "other right" of private self-help and self-control regarding an intimate sphere of private life? Could the formula be generalized beyond birth control to other areas, or is birth control *sui generis?*

Approached from a slightly different standpoint, is not the ninth amendment concept of rights retained by the people well adapted to support a constitutional policy of confining the privacy invasions authorized by other constitutional processes to the bare minimum necessary to accomplish valid social ends?[77]

Suffice it to say for the present that unless some kind of information-access theory is recognized as implicit in *Griswold*, then it stands as a decision without a satisfying rationale. At least it will stand thus except for those who can join the Court in using the ploy of

---

77. There may be some unarticulated privacy aspects in Estes v. Texas, 381 U.S. 532 (1965), decided the same day as *Griswold*, in which a conviction was reversed because the trial had been televised. Except for a passing mention in the Brief of the Petitioner, pp. 16-18, and Mr. Justice Clark's statement in his opinion for the Court that televised trial coverage "is a form of mental—if not physical—harassment" of the defendant (381 U.S. at 549), the primary focus in the briefs and opinions was on denial of a fair trial because of the impact of television. See also Brief of American Civil Liberties Union and the Texas Civil Liberties Union as Amici Curiae; Brief of the American Bar Association as Amicus Curiae. And yet could it not be argued, consistently with the result in *Estes*, that even though a trial is not a secret place, there is a ninth amendment "other right" of a defendant not to have his public courtroom trial transformed into a public television spectacle?

"standing" to re-make the actual birth-control-clinic situation into a marital-use-of-contraceptives situation. With the issue thus re-made, we have a modern morality play, with much judicial finger-shaking at fictional police invading a fictional bedchamber of a fictional couple in search of evidence of the use of contraceptives. The actual result of *Griswold* may be applauded, but to reach this result was it necessary to play charades with the Constitution?

NINE JUSTICES IN SEARCH OF A DOCTRINE

Thomas I. Emerson*

T HE case of *Griswold v. Connecticut,*[1] like few others in recent
times, presented the United States Supreme Court with a hope-
lessly unsupportable piece of state legislation and an unusual variety
of possible doctrinal solutions. The Court's response to this situation,
and the implications of its choice of doctrine for the future of
individual rights in America, make an intriguing study of the judicial process.

The Connecticut law, as a matter of social policy, had little or
nothing to be said for it. It was enacted in 1879 and remained as a
relic of a Comstockian philosophy which had long since ceased to
be widely held, if it ever had been. The statute was at war with all
accepted standards of medical practice. It invaded the sacred realm
of marital privacy, and for all practical purposes denied to married
couples the right of deciding whether or when to have children.
Under certain not infrequent circumstances, it imposed upon individuals the cruel choice between sexual abstinence on the one hand
and ill health, death, or deformed children on the other. Not generally enforced, indeed unenforceable in most instances, it hung like a
cloud over the medical profession. More important, its enforcement
only against birth control clinics resulted in patent discrimination
against persons who were too poor or too uneducated to seek private
medical advice. Its basic purpose was fantastically in conflict with
the clearly perceived need to deal with the world's second most
critical problem—the population explosion. Even its staunchest
supporter, the Roman Catholic Church, was ready to concede that
the use of contraceptives by married couples involved a religious
principle rather than a public policy to be imposed on all faiths by
government sanction. Yet the legislature failed to repeal the statute.[2]

To the ordinary layman, *Griswold v. Connecticut* seemed easy.
But to the lawyer it was somewhat more difficult. The lawyer's
problem with the case was that the issues did not readily fit into

---

* Professor of Law, Yale University.—Ed. The author wishes to point out that
he was one of the counsel for appellants in the case of *Griswold v. Connecticut.* This
article is written in the capacity of law professor rather than advocate, but the bias
should be noted.

1. 381 U.S. 479 (1965).

2. There is some evidence that, at least when the case was in its final stages before
the Supreme Court, many Connecticut legislators preferred to have the Court, rather
than themselves, make the decision to eliminate the statute.

any existing legal pigeonhole. Actually, there were five possibilities. The case could have been dealt with under the equal protection clause, the first amendment, substantive due process, the right of privacy, or, *in extremis*, the ninth amendment. In order to strike down the statute under any of these doctrines, however, the Court would be forced to enter uncharted waters. Whatever course the Court took, its action was bound to be pregnant with possibilities crucial to the development of the law in a vital area of American life.

I.   EQUAL PROTECTION

The primary equal protection issue arose out of the fact, already mentioned, that although the Connecticut birth control law was a dead letter as far as private physicians and individuals were concerned, it was effectively enforced against birth control clinics. Thus, in actual operation the law did not apply to the private sector of medical practice but did restrict the public sector, thereby discriminating against persons of low income or little education. A subsidiary equal protection issue was that the law, in effect, favored unmarried persons as against married couples. Contraceptives could be legally sold in Connecticut for prevention of disease; faithful partners to a marriage would have no occasion to use them for such purposes, whereas unmarried persons could legally do so. The same factors favored persons engaging in extramarital relations.

Appellants did not rely on the equal protection argument as such, although they did urge it upon the Court as an element of substantive due process. At the very opening of oral argument, however, Mr. Justice Brennan raised the issue, and other Justices indicated their interest in it. Similarly, Mr. Justice White, in his concurring opinion, although proceeding primarily on due process grounds, stressed that "a statute with these effects bears a substantial burden of justification when attacked under the Fourteenth Amendment," citing three equal protection cases.[3]

The problem posed is a far-reaching one. The Court has of course employed the equal protection clause, with increasing refinements and elaboration, in the area of race relations. The important question is how much further the Court will go in utilizing this constitutional provision to aid the economically and socially disadvantaged. The Court is steadily moving in that direction. Already it has insisted upon eliminating some of the effects of gross disparity in

---

3. 381 U.S. at 503. The equal protection cases cited, along with a due process case, were McLaughlin v. Florida, 379 U.S. 184 (1964); Skinner v. Oklahoma, 316 U.S. 535 (1942); Yick Wo v. Hopkins, 118 U.S. 356 (1886).

income between defendants caught in the criminal process,[4] it has invoked the equal protection clause to achieve political equality in reapportionment cases,[5] and it has relied upon the clause to protect a business enterprise against economic grudge legislation.[6] As the war against poverty demonstrates, few issues are of more importance to the society of the future than that of assisting its disadvantaged members.

However, the development of equal protection along these lines raises a host of obvious difficulties. It will not be easy to reconcile such equal protection theories with the economic and social laissez-faire assumptions and practices upon which our society has operated over many years and to which it still largely adheres. These uncertainties persuaded counsel for the appellants that there was little to gain in raising bare equal protection issues, as distinct from substantive due process issues, in this litigation. Under the circumstances, the Court, probably wisely, refrained from probing further. However, the interest in the issue evidenced by some members of the Court carries a portent for the future.

II. THE FIRST AMENDMENT

The first amendment issue was raised by appellants, but it was relatively weak. It was quite evident that appellants had engaged in some conduct—such as giving physical examinations and dispensing contraceptives—which could be classified only as action rather than speech. Their argument conceded this point, but stressed two other factors. First, the aiding and abetting statute, under which appellants were actually convicted, made it a crime not only to "assist" and "abet" another person to commit an offense, but also to "counsel" him to do so. Thus, at least in theory and possible application, this statutory provision swept broadly into the first amendment area. Second, in the conduct of the trial no effort had been made to distinguish between protected areas of speech and unprotected areas of action; everything was mixed together in one grab bag.

The case thus involved two crucial aspects of first amendment theory. One concerns the coverage of the first amendment—the extent to which it protects conduct that is not strictly speech but is essential to the exercise of free speech. The other, closely related, is the problem of separating speech from action in a complex situa-

4. See, *e.g.*, Griffin v. Illinois, 351 U.S. 12 (1956).
5. See, *e.g.*, Baker v. Carr, 369 U.S. 186 (1962).
6. See Morey v. Doud, 354 U.S. 457 (1957).

tion, rather than lumping them together in a way which penalizes speech in the course of regulating action. The Court has come more and more to recognize these problems and has begun to deal with them.[7] In view of the multiplying indirect restrictions upon speech, these questions are bound to become key issues in our effort to maintain a system of freedom of expression.

The birth control case, however, did not present a very favorable opportunity for the Court to press forward on these frontiers. The Court would have had to go beyond anything it had decided before, and it would have had to face some hard problems in determining how far to cut down aiding and abetting statutes and, indeed, much legislation dealing with inchoate crimes. Although the Court refrained from treating first amendment problems directly, first amendment overtones were strongly heard in the prevailing opinion of Mr. Justice Douglas. It would seem clear that any state law applied to prohibit the giving of advice on the value or methods of contraception would fall under the ban of the first amendment. More important, while there is nothing in the opinions on the question of separating speech from action, the Douglas opinion does continue the dialogue on the issue of first amendment coverage.

III.   SUBSTANTIVE DUE PROCESS

Substantive due process issues were central to the case. Not only was the direct argument strongly urged, but due process considerations were also involved in the right of privacy issue, to be discussed later.

The space available here does not permit a detailed analysis of the Connecticut law or its operation, beyond what has already been undertaken. Suffice it to say that a factual demonstration that the law was arbitrary, unreasonable, capricious, and not reasonably related to a proper legislative purpose, did not pose serious difficulties. This feature of the case was the basis for lay optimism over the outcome. The due process argument was facilitated, moreover, by the fact that neither the Connecticut legislature nor the courts had ever fully articulated, much less defended, the objectives of the legislature in enacting the law. Starting from this point, however, there were two aspects of due process which raised significant ques-

---

7. With respect to the coverage of the first amendment, see NAACP v. Button, 371 U.S. 415 (1963). With respect to the separation of speech and action, see Gibson v. Legislative Investigation Comm., 372 U.S. 539 (1963). For a further discussion of these matters, see Emerson, *Freedom of Association and Freedom of Expression*, 74 YALE L.J. 1, 24-32 (1964).

tions. The first was whether the Court would undertake to elaborate a distinction between the application of substantive due process to cases involving personal rights and its application to cases concerning economic rights. The second involved the question as to what standards of due process are to be employed in considering legislation based not on objective facts related to the public welfare, but rather on grounds of purely moral principle.

A. *Substantive Due Process and the Distinction Between Personal and Economic Rights*

In the development of substantive due process, attention has been primarily focused upon cases where the doctrine has been invoked in opposition to economic or social welfare legislation. The earlier cases, in which due process was freely employed to strike down such legislation, are typified by *Lochner v. New York.*[8] However, beginning in the middle thirties with *Nebbia v. New York*[9] and *West Coast Hotel Co. v. Parrish*,[10] the Court sharply shifted direction, and since that time it has been virtually unwilling to listen to the due process argument in such cases.[11] At the same time, there has been developing another line of cases in which due process is utilized on behalf of individual òr personal rights. This second line of authority commenced with *Meyer v. Nebraska*,[12] in which the Court held invalid a state statute prohibiting the teaching of the German language to pupils who had not passed the eighth grade, and *Pierce v. Society of Sisters*,[13] in which the Court ruled unconstitutional a law preventing the operation of private schools. The *Meyer* and *Pierce* decisions, in which Mr. Justice McReynolds wrote for the Court, did not distinguish between personal and economic rights, and the decisions in fact leaned heavily upon the need for protecting property rights. Nevertheless, the distinction is implicit.

More recently, the Court has expressly employed the due process doctrine to uphold individual rights in a variety of cases. One example of this approach is *Wieman v. Updegraff*,[14] in which a state loyalty program that penalized innocent membership in a "sub-

---

8. 198 U.S. 45 (1905).
9. 291 U.S. 502 (1934).
10. 300 U.S. 379 (1937).
11. See, *e.g.*, Ferguson v. Skrupa, 372 U.S. 726 (1963); Williamson v. Lee Optical Co., 348 U.S. 483 (1955); Berman v. Parker, 348 U.S. 26 (1954); Lincoln Fed. Labor Union v. Northwestern Iron & Metal Co., 335 U.S. 525 (1949).
12. 262 U.S. 390 (1923).
13. 268 U.S. 510 (1925).
14. 344 U.S. 183 (1952).

versive" organization was found to be invalid. Other cases have invoked the doctrines of undue breadth or vagueness, which are mixed concepts of procedural and substantive due process, to strike down similar legislation.[15] In *Aptheker v. Secretary of State*[16] a federal statute denying passports to members of the Communist Party was held unconstitutional on the ground that it was not narrowly drafted to meet a specific evil. Yet the Court has never fully articulated the reasons for the difference in its approach to these two lines of cases.

The distinction is nevertheless a fundamental one. In the *Meyer-Aptheker* type of case, the legislation touches upon fundamental individual and personal rights essential to maintaining the independence, integrity, and private development of a citizen in a highly organized, yet democratic society. In the *Lochner-Nebbia* situation, the legislation deals with economic regulation of commercial and property rights, essential to maintaining the public interest in controlling a highly complex, industrialized society. The distinction is thus basic in striking the balance between public interest and private right in a modern, technologically developed nation.

The Connecticut birth control case would have been an opportune one in which to clarify due process doctrine along the lines indicated. But the Court chose not to rest its decision on straight due process grounds and hence never reached these issues directly. However, there is language in the opinions which indicates that a majority of the Court are ready to apply the distinction. Mr. Justice Douglas stated in the prevailing opinion:

> We do not sit as a super-legislature to determine the wisdom, need, and propriety of laws that touch economic problems, business affairs, or social conditions. This law, however, operates directly on an intimate relation of husband and wife and their physician's role in one aspect of that relation.[17]

Mr. Justice Goldberg, concurring for himself and Mr. Chief Justice Warren and Mr. Justice Brennan, was even more explicit:

> In a long series of cases this Court has held that where fundamental personal liberties are involved, they may not be abridged by the States simply on a showing that a regulatory statute has some rational relationship to the effectuation of

---

15. See, *e.g.*, Baggett v. Bullitt, 377 U.S. 360 (1964); NAACP v. Alabama *ex rel.* Flowers, 377 U.S. 288 (1964); Cramp v. Board of Public Instruction, 368 U.S. 278 (1961); Louisiana *ex rel.* Gremillion v. NAACP, 366 U.S. 293 (1961); Shelton v. Tucker, 364 U.S. 479 (1960).
16. 378 U.S. 500 (1964).
17. 381 U.S. at 482.

a proper state purpose. "Where there is a significant encroach-ment upon personal liberty, the State may prevail only upon showing a subordinating interest which is compelling," *Bates v. Little Rock*, 361 U.S. 516, 524. The law must be shown "necessary, and not merely rationally related, to the accomplish-ment of a permissible state policy." *McLaughlin v. Florida*, 379 U.S. 184, 196.[18]

Mr. Justice White, alone among the majority, placed his decision squarely upon substantive due process grounds. The opinion is a narrow one, however, taking advantage of a concession made by counsel for Connecticut at oral argument that the sole purpose of the law was to prevent "promiscuous or illicit sexual relationships." Mr. Justice White did not have much trouble demolishing this position, and hence did not find it necessary to enter into more subtle analysis of the due process clause.

Mr. Justice Black and Mr. Justice Stewart did face the issue, however, and explicitly repudiated any distinction between the two types of due process cases. In fact, both Justices went farther, arguing that substantive due process should be limited to the issue of whether the legislation was unduly vague.[19] The majority, it is clear, did not hold either view. It can be expected, therefore, that at some future time the distinction between personal rights and economic rights in the application of due process doctrine will be more fully elaborated.

B. *Substantive Due Process and Its Relation to Public Morals*

The second significant aspect of substantive due process arose out of the fact that the primary objective of the Connecticut statute, as far as could be determined, was to promote public morality by prohibiting the use of extrinsic devices to prevent conception, even within the marital relation.[20] The enactment was, in other words, designed to compel adherence to a purely moral principle. Thus, to attack such legislation on due process grounds posed a special problem.

When legislation is designed to promote health, safety, or the

18. *Id.* at 497. It should be noted that Mr. Justice Goldberg was applying first amendment and racial-equal protection doctrine to issues of substantive due process.

19. *Id.* at 511-18, 520-24, 528.

20. As noted above, counsel for Connecticut apparently abandoned this position at the oral argument, and Justices White and Goldberg relied upon this concession. Never-theless, this seems to be the position taken by the Connecticut courts. See *State v. Nelson*, 126 Conn. 412, 424, 11 A.2d 856, 861 (1940).

general welfare in a material sense, its validity under the due process clause can be tested by considerations that can be objectively determined and rationally weighed. The questions whether the statute is arbitrary or capricious, or has a reasonable relation to a proper legislative purpose, turn in such cases upon factual material which can be discovered and presented to the court and upon value judgments which are subject to exposition and debate. The Brandeis brief is, of course, a classic illustration of this approach to the due process clause.

When the legislation is designed to promote public morality, however, the problem of applying the standards of due process may take a different form. In some cases, such as a statute prohibiting prostitution, the moral purposes may be justified by reference to objective and rational factors relevant to the promotion of the general welfare. However, in other cases the legislature may undertake to legislate purely on the basis of moral principles which are not subject to objective evaluation. In such a case, how are the customary criteria of due process to be applied?

Justices Black and Stewart, as indicated above, would not attempt to apply substantive due process standards, other than vagueness, at all. But the other Justices repudiate this approach. Hence they cannot take the position that the simple claim of a moral aim by the legislature satisfies the requirement of due process. Any such a doctrine would immunize virtually all legislation from the mandate of the due process clause. It would allow the legislatures to impose restraints upon individual liberties solely on the ground that some insignificant fraction of the community regarded the issue as a moral one. Yet a law prohibiting women from appearing in public without veils or forbidding women to use lipstick or cosmetics, even though some persons in the community might regard such practices as immoral, would surely be held an arbitrary infringement of personal liberty outlawed by the due process clause. What, then, should be the constitutional standards for applying the due process clause in cases where the legislature seeks to promote public morals?

Counsel for appellants argued that the standard in such cases should at least be that (1) the moral practices regulated by the statute must be objectively related to the public welfare, or (2) in the event no such relationship can be demonstrated, the regulation must conform to the predominant view of morality in the community. In other words, if the legislature cannot establish that the law promotes the public welfare in a material sense, it cannot enforce the morality of a minority group upon other members of the community. The obscenity cases were cited as supporting a somewhat similar doctrine. It was further suggested that the first standard set forth above would be sufficient in itself, without the second. That is, if the moral principles cannot be objectively related to the public welfare, the legislation fails, for that reason alone, to meet the standards of due process. However, it was pointed out that it was not necessary to take this position in order to decide the case then before the Court.

Mr. Justice Stewart, although not meeting this argument squarely, apparently considered and rejected it.[21] The other Justices did not refer to it. Obviously the problem raises crucial but controversial questions respecting the relation of law and morals. The Court was not willing to venture into such a delicate area. Perhaps one cannot blame them.

IV. NINTH AMENDMENT

The ninth amendment issue was not raised at the trial by the appellants, and was urged in the Supreme Court only as one source of the right of privacy. However, to the astonishment of many observers, five of the Justices accepted the invitation to consider the ninth amendment as a basis for invalidating the Connecticut statute. Mr. Justice Douglas invoked it as one of the constitutional guarantees from which the right of privacy was derived. Mr. Justice Goldberg discussed it at length, but his opinion seems to give it a more limited significance. He expressly repudiated the argument that the ninth amendment "constitutes an independent source of rights protected from infringement by either the States or the Federal Government."[22] Rather, his position was that "the Ninth Amendment shows a belief of the Constitution's authors that fundamental rights exist that are not expressly enumerated in the first eight amendments and an intent that the list of rights included there not be deemed exhaustive."[23] The specific rights must therefore still be derived from other sources.

The fact that a majority of the Supreme Court, for the first time, relied upon the ninth amendment in any serious way to strike down state legislation is an event of considerable importance. Yet there remains grave doubt that the ninth amendment has a significant future. Mr. Justice Goldberg's formulation does not seem to open

21. 381 U.S. at 530.
22. *Id.* at 492.
23. *Ibid.*

any really new possibilities. The doctrine that the due process clause protects certain fundamental rights not expressly mentioned in the Bill of Rights or elsewhere in the Constitution is well established, and has been utilized on many other occasions.[24] Mr. Justice Douglas' use of the ninth amendment carries a greater potential. Under his theory, the ninth amendment might be utilized to expand the concept of privacy or, perhaps, to guarantee other basic rights. It would hardly be surprising, however, if this development were some decades away.

V.   THE RIGHT OF PRIVACY

Since no constitutional "right of privacy" had previously been recognized, at least as an independent doctrine, in order to dispose of the case on this ground it was necessary to establish a new constitutional concept. This involved three major problems. One was to determine the source from which the new doctrine was derived, a second was to indicate the standards by which the doctrine would be applied, and the third was to suggest, if only tentatively, the scope of its application.

A.   *The Creation of the Right*

With respect to the initial problem of determining the source of the right of privacy, there were two approaches available. The first was to argue that, although the Constitution nowhere refers in express terms to a right of privacy, nevertheless various provisions of the Constitution embody separate aspects of such a concept, and the composite of these protections should be accorded the status of a recognized constitutional right. This approach was adopted in the prevailing opinion of Mr. Justice Douglas: "Specific guarantees in the Bill of Rights have penumbras, formed by emanations from those guarantees that help give them life and substance."[25] From the first amendment, the third amendment, the fourth amendment, the privilege against self-incrimination of the fifth amendment, and the ninth amendment, he concluded that "the right of privacy which presses for recognition here is a legitimate one."[26]

The second approach starts from the position that the due process clause of the fourteenth amendment, whether or not it incorporates some or all of the provisions of the Bill of Rights, guarantees

24. Mr. Justice Goldberg himself cites, among other cases, Aptheker v. Secretary of State, 378 U.S. 500 (1964), and Bolling v. Sharpe, 347 U.S. 497 (1954).
25. 381 U.S. at 484.
26. *Id.* at 485.

such basic rights as are "implicit in the concept of ordered liberty." The right of privacy can be considered such a fundamental right and hence protected under the due process clause. This view of the matter was taken by Mr. Justice Harlan in his concurring opinion.[27]

Mr. Justice Goldberg, in his opinion joined by the Chief Justice and Mr. Justice Brennan, seems to have combined both approaches. He expressly accepted Mr. Justice Douglas' view that a right of privacy was "protected, as being within the protected penumbra of specific guarantees of the Bill of Rights."[28] However, he also pointed out that "the concept of liberty protects those personal rights that are fundamental, and is not confined to the specific terms of the Bill of Rights."[29] He, too, went on to find that the right of privacy was a fundamental right.

The precise source of the right of privacy is not as important as the fact that six Justices found such a right to exist, and thereby established it for the first time as an independent constitutional right. It was a bold innovation. Yet it was not entirely without precedent. The Court had previously recognized a somewhat similar "right of association" derived from the various specific guarantees of freedom of speech, press, assembly, and petition in the first amendment.[30]

In any event, the creation of a right to privacy is a step with enormous consequences. The concept of limited government has always included the idea that governmental powers stop short of certain intrusions into the personal life of the citizen. This is indeed one of the basic distinctions between absolute and limited government. Ultimate and pervasive control of the individual, in all aspects of his life, is the hallmark of the absolute state. In contrast, a system of limited government safeguards a private sector, which belongs to the individual, firmly distinguishing it from the public sector, which the state can control. Protection of this private sector—protection, in other words, of the dignity and integrity of the individual —has become increasingly important as modern society has developed. All the forces of a technological age—industrialization, urbanization, and organization—operate to narrow the area of privacy and facilitate intrusions into it. In modern terms, the capacity to maintain and support this enclave of private life marks the difference between a democratic and a totalitarian society.

---

27. *Id.* at 500. Mr. Justice Harlan's views are stated at greater length in his dissenting opinion at a prior stage of the litigation. See Poe v. Ullman, 367 U.S. 497, 522 (1961).

28. 381 U.S. at 487.

29. *Id.* at 486.

30. See the line of cases beginning with NAACP v. Alabama *ex rel.* Patterson, 357 U.S. 449 (1958), collected in Emerson, *supra* note 7, at 6-15.

B. *Standards of Application*

Having established the constitutional right of privacy, the Court was confronted with the second problem—determination of the standards by which the new doctrine would be applied. Mr. Justice Douglas dealt with this question somewhat summarily. He noted that the Connecticut law, "in forbidding the *use* of contraceptives rather than regulating their manufacture or sale, seeks to achieve its goals by means having a maximum destructive impact upon [the marriage] relationship."[31] He mentioned specifically the problem of actual enforcement, of allowing the police "to search the sacred precincts of marital bedrooms for telltale signs of the use of contraceptives."[32] He also applied the rule against undue breadth: "Such a law cannot stand in light of the familiar principle, so often applied by this Court, that a 'governmental purpose to control or prevent activities constitutionally subject to state regulation may not be achieved by means which sweep unnecessarily broadly and thereby invade the area of protected freedoms.' "[33]

The Goldberg opinion proceeded in a somewhat different direction. It took as its primary standard a balancing test, but one which placed a heavy burden of justification upon the government: "[T]he State may prevail only upon showing a subordinating interest which is compelling."[34] Mr. Justice Goldberg also reiterated the Douglas position that the law must not "sweep unnecessarily broadly," and added that other Connecticut laws on adultery and fornication "demonstrate that means for achieving the same basic purpose of protecting marital fidelity are available to Connecticut without the need to 'invade the area of protected freedoms.' "[35]

While the Court is thus not settled upon the exact formula by which to determine whether the right of privacy has been infringed, it would seem clear that the test is more severe than that applied in substantive due process cases involving economic regulation. On the other hand, in view of the newness of the constitutional right, the vagueness of the concept, and the general lack of precise standards, it would appear that there is little prospect of working out any such strict test as has been proposed for first amendment cases. It is most likely that future decisions will follow the Goldberg ap-

---

31. 381 U.S. at 485.
32. *Ibid.*
33. *Ibid.* Mr. Justice Douglas had previously elaborated his views in Poe v. Ullman, 367 U.S. 497 (1961), where he had also stressed primarily the impact of enforcement activities upon marital privacy.
34. 381 U.S. at 497.
35. *Id.* at 497-98.

proach—a balancing of factors, with the government required to show a "compelling interest," supplemented by doctrines of undue breadth, vagueness, and the feasibility of alternative measures.

C. *The Scope of the Right*

With respect to the third problem—the scope of the right of privacy—the Court proceeded with its customary caution when venturing into new fields. The facts of the case before it, although strong, embraced a relatively narrow area. They were confined to a *use* statute, discriminatory in operation, which had been applied to married couples. The Douglas opinion, to the extent it deals specifically with the scope of the right to privacy, treats only of the "marriage relationship." The Goldberg opinion is also addressed to the "right of marital privacy," although it does refer to the privacy of "the marital home" and the right "to marry and raise a family." It is conceivable that in future cases the Court will limit the doctrine to the marriage relationship, or even refuse to extend it beyond the precise facts of the Connecticut case. However, such an outcome seems unlikely, since constitutional doctrines have a way of expanding beyond the boundaries of the original case. This is especially true where, as here, the right established is one which responds so acutely to the growing needs of the society. It is impossible to foretell, of course, what the future course of development may be. But it is not hard to anticipate some of the claims that will be pressed upon the Court in the coming years. And any appraisal of the significance of the Court's action in the Connecticut case demands some speculation, however brief and uncertain, concerning the Court's response.

One series of issues revolves around the same aspect of the right to privacy as that involved in *Griswold*—the marital relationship. It would seem reasonably clear that other laws attempting to prohibit certain kinds of sexual activity by married couples, such as so-called acts of "perversion," requiring a type of enforcement similar to that implicit in the Connecticut statute, would fall under the ban against invasion of privacy. Less clear, however, is the fate of state laws regulating not the use of contraceptive devices, but their manufacture, sale, or distribution. Plainly, many forms of regulation— such as those designed to safeguard health or safety, or requiring distribution through physicians or licensed drug stores—would be upheld. But would an attempt by the state to enforce a total prohibition of access to contraceptives by married couples, such as the

Massachusetts statute,[36] constitute an invasion of the right of marital privacy? In this situation, the nature of the right is not coterminous with that protected in the *Griswold* case. It no longer involves those aspects of police enforcement which loomed so large under the Connecticut statute. Rather it consists primarily in the right to have or not have children, and to plan a family. In view of Mr. Justice Goldberg's inclusion of the "right to marry and raise a family" within the right of privacy, and in view of the fundamental nature of such a right, it would not be surprising if the Court accepted such a claim.

If this supposition is accurate, then the corollary would seem to follow that action by the government to compel limitation of births, at least in the absence of special compelling circumstances, would also constitute an invasion of privacy. Indeed, Mr. Justice Goldberg stated this as an a fortiori proposition. The new doctrine thus carries serious implications for sterilization laws and future birth control programs. Undoubtedly the government could encourage birth control by many means other than strict compulsion, but a line between encouragement and coercion would have to be worked out. On the same view of the scope of the right to privacy, the way would be open for an attack upon significant aspects of the abortion laws.

An additional area in which claims to the right of privacy are likely to be invoked embraces the multitude of existing laws relating to sexual conduct outside the marital relation. It seems unlikely that the Court would disturb most of the legislation relating to adultery, fornication (commercial or otherwise), and homosexuality. Indeed, Justices Goldberg and Harlan expressly disclaimed any such intention. However, some of the particularly arbitrary, irrational, or unenforceable aspects of such legislation might be vulnerable. It is conceivable that sometime in the future, as mores change and knowledge of the problem grows, all sexual activities of two consenting adults in private will be brought within the right of privacy.

Apart from sex laws, it would not be surprising to see the concept of privacy employed in a number of other situations to safeguard the private sector of our lives from government encroachment. One obvious area in which this concept is sure to be pressed and may well be successful, at least in part, is electronic eavesdropping. The scientific possibilities are so fantastic and the invasion of privacy

---

36. MASS. GEN. LAWS ch. 272, § 21 (1932).

so devastating that it is hard to believe a civilized society will not feel compelled to throw up some protection to individuals. This may come about through legislation, but the constitutional right of privacy could also play a significant role.[37]

Other such areas also come to mind. Various kinds of police practices, not technically covered by the search and seizure guarantees of the fourth amendment, would easily fall within an expanding concept of the right to privacy.[38] Efforts by government officials to compel the production of private information through legislative committees, lie-detector tests, or other similar means may gradually be brought within the constitutional doctrine. Release of official records of arrests not resulting in conviction might be curtailed. Finally, the whole field of social welfare legislation and administration may be forced into procedures and practices more compatible with human dignity and integrity. Thus, restrictions imposed by official or semi-official welfare agencies upon the private life or activities of welfare recipients may well become subject to the new guarantees of privacy.[39]

The foregoing observations are merely indicative of some of the areas that may be encompassed within an expanded concept of the right to privacy. Undoubtedly the Court will proceed slowly, developing the right to privacy on a case-by-case basis. The essential point is that the key constitutional doctrine has been enunciated, and many forces in our society will press hard toward fuller realization of its great potential.

VI. Conclusion

What, then, are we to conclude about the Court's performance in the birth control case? On the whole, the Court's choice of the privacy doctrine as the basis of its decision seems sound. Unprecedented as it was, and as broad and ill-defined as it remains, the doctrine still represents the narrowest and most precise formula available, and the one most relevant to the issues presented. This

---

37. See, *e.g.*, Judge Washington's dissent in Silverman v. United States, 275 F.2d 173, 178 (D.C. Cir. 1960).

38. It should be noted that to the extent specific activities of government officials are held to violate the constitutional right of privacy, they may be subject to criminal prosecution and civil redress under federal civil rights legislation. See, *e.g.*, York v. Story, 324 F.2d 450 (9th Cir. 1963), holding that allegations that police officers took photographs of a woman complainant in the nude and distributed them among their fellow officers stated a cause of action under REV. STAT. § 1979 (1875), 42 U.S.C. § 1983 (1964).

39. See Reich, *Individual Rights and Social Welfare—The Emerging Legal Issues*, 74 YALE L.J. 1245 (1965).

creation of a new constitutional protection meets a critical need of society, and the new doctrine seems to have a viable and significant future.

The Court will undoubtedly be attacked upon the broader ground that, since the objections to the Connecticut law did not fall clearly within any established and specific legal category, the Court should not have invalidated the law. at all. Supporters of the argument for "neutral principles" can hardly be satisfied that the creation of a new principle conforms to their view of the Court's function. Furthermore, the concern of Mr. Justice Black, forcefully expressed in his dissent, that more is to be gained by strict adherence to specific provisions of the Constitution than by excursions into the realm of "natural law," cannot be discarded lightly. Yet it is significant that Mr. Justice Harlan, the most ardent advocate of judicial self-restraint now on the Court, joined in the establishment of the new constitutional right to privacy. This indicates that, in the context of the case before it, the claim to constitutional protection presented could not readily be thrust aside. In any event, the role of the Court as guardian of individual rights has been both solidified and advanced.

PENUMBRAS, PERIPHERIES, EMANATIONS, THINGS FUNDAMENTAL AND THINGS FORGOTTEN: THE *GRISWOLD* CASE

*Paul G. Kauper**

Griswold v. Connecticut[1] held by a seven-to-two margin that the Connecticut criminal statute forbidding the use of contraceptive devices by married couples was unconstitutional under the fourteenth amendment. This simplified version of the holding, however, does not adequately portray the great variety of doctrines relied upon by the Justices constituting the majority. The opinion of the Court, written by Mr. Justice Douglas, found the statute invalid because it invaded a constitutionally protected right of marital privacy found to emanate from the specific provisions of the Bill of Rights and made applicable to the states by the fourteenth amendment. The separate opinion by Mr. Justice Goldberg, joined by Mr. Chief Justice Warren and Mr. Justice Brennan, expressed concurrence in Mr. Justice Douglas' opinion and then proceeded to an independent ground—that the right of privacy as invoked and protected in this case is a fundamental right protected by the due process clause against state deprivation. The opinion used the ninth amendment to help bolster the independent fundamental rights theory. The separate concurring opinion by Mr. Justice Harlan, incorporating views expressed earlier in a dissenting opinion,[2] clearly disassociated itself from the opinion of the Court and rested squarely on the proposition that the Connecticut statute intruded into the privacy of married couples, thereby impairing a fundamental right protected by the due process clause of the fourteenth amendment. Mr. Justice White, writing a separate concurring opinion, likewise explicitly rested his case on the due process clause, finding that the Connecticut statute as applied to married couples deprived them of liberty without due process of law, since it invaded the right to be free from regulation of the intimacies of the marriage relationship. The dissenting opinions by Justices Black and Stewart rejected the notion that the "right of privacy" on which the case turned finds support in the specifics of the Bill of Rights, and further rejected the idea that the Court is free, in the interpretation of the due process clause of the fourteenth amendment, to formulate a conception of fundamental rights having no foundation in the specific guarantees of the Constitution.

* Henry M. Butzel Professor of Law, University of Michigan.—Ed.
1. 381 U.S. 479 (1965).
2. Poe v. Ullman, 367 U.S. 597 (1961).

This brief introductory statement is sufficient to point up the fascinating feature of *Griswold*: it laid bare the basic differences within the Court respecting its role in the protection of fundamental rights and respecting the interrelationship of the fourteenth amendment and the Bill of Rights as a central aspect of this problem. It is to these aspects of the case that my comments are directed.[3]

The varying theories followed in the several opinions in the *Griswold* case can be fully understood and appreciated only in the context of the tortuous but fascinating history of the judicial interpretation of the fourteenth amendment.

I. FUNDAMENTAL RIGHTS AND THEIR RELATIONSHIP TO THE BILL OF RIGHTS

By the end of the nineteenth century the Supreme Court had committed itself to an interpretation of the due process clause whereby the clause was enlarged beyond its original connotation of procedural regularity and converted into a vehicle for protecting the so-called fundamental rights.[4] In the twentieth century the Court has used various expressions to describe its understanding of fundamental rights: they are the rights implicit in those "fundamental principles of liberty and justice which lie at the base of all our civil and political institutions";[5] they are those rights "so rooted in the traditions and conscience of our people as to be ranked as fundamental."[6] In his classic opinion for the Court in *Palko v. Connecticut*,[7] Mr. Justice Cardozo spoke of the rights "implicit in the concept of ordered liberty."[8] The rights protected as fundamental include both procedural and substantive rights. As applied in its earlier stages, the due process clause as the guarantee of procedural rights centered on the "fair trial" concept.[9] The substantive rights emphasized in the earlier stages of the development of the clause were liberty of contract and freedom in the enjoyment and use of property. These eventually suffered a decline in the degree of

---

3. The editors requested me to give my interpretation and comments respecting the *Griswold* decision. No attempt is made here to deal at length with the issues and questions to which the comments are directed or to call the reader's attention to the voluminous literature on these matters. The documentation is on the whole limited to the necessary case citations.

4. See, *e.g.*, Allgeyer v. Louisiana, 165 U.S. 578 (1897).

5. Hebert v. Louisiana, 272 U.S. 312, 316 (1926).

6. Snyder v. Massachusetts, 291 U.S. 97, 105 (1934).

7. 302 U.S. 319 (1937).

8. *Id.* at 325. For a collection of phrases used by the Court in formulating the fundamental rights theory, see Mr. Justice Black's dissenting opinion in *Griswold*, 381 U.S. at 511-12 n.4.

9. See, *e.g.*, Palko v. Connecticut, 302 U.S. 319 (1937); Hurtado v. California, 110 U.S. 516 (1884).

judicial protection received, but in their place the Court later stressed the freedoms specifically set forth in the first amendment—the freedoms of religion, speech, press and assembly.[10]

A notable and controversial aspect of this development was the Court's recognition that the fundamental rights protected under the due process clause of the fourteenth amendment had no necessary relationship to the specifics set forth in the first eight amendments as restrictions on the federal government. In other words, the Court rejected the idea that the effect of the fourteenth amendment was to make the first eight amendments apply to the states. In his opinion in *Palko*, Mr. Justice Cardozo said that the due process clause absorbed the specifics of the Bill of Rights only insofar as they were "of the very essence of a scheme of ordered liberty."[11] Indeed, the whole process whereby the freedoms of the first amendment were incorporated into the fourteenth amendment as fundamental rights was a clear-cut application of substantive due process concepts. The end result has been that the Court has, on the one hand, rejected certain specifics catalogued in the first eight amendments as nonfundamental and has, on the other hand, recognized as fundamental certain liberties not specified in these amendments.

To state these developments in what may be called the "main line" in the interpretation of the fourteenth amendment is not to suggest that they have gone unchallenged. The elder Mr. Justice Harlan dissented from the proposition that the rights protected under the first eight amendments were not included in the rights protected under the due process clause.[12] Mr. Justice Holmes spearheaded a group of dissenters who remonstrated against the use of the due process clause to invalidate state legislation found to be an interference with liberty of contract.[13] Mr. Justice Black, joined by Mr. Justice Douglas, forcibly stated in his dissenting opinion in *Adamson v. California*[14] his objections to the fundamental rights interpretation, which he equated with natural law thinking. In his view the effect of the fourteenth amendment was to make the Bill of Rights apply to the states, but the Court could not use the due process clause as a vehicle for protecting any other rights on the theory that they were fundamental. Justices Murphy and Rutledge, in their dissents in *Adamson*, had agreed that the specifics of the Bill of Rights ap-

10. For references to the cases and a review of this development, see KAUPER, FRONTIERS OF CONSTITUTIONAL LIBERTY 18-54 (1956).

11. Palko v. Connecticut, 302 U.S. 319, 325 (1937).

12. See Twining v. New Jersey, 211 U.S. 78 (1908) (dissenting opinion); Hurtado v. California, 110 U.S. 516 (1884) (dissenting opinion).

13. Lochner v. New York, 198 U.S. 45 (1905) (dissenting opinion).

14. 332 U.S. 46 (1947).

plied to the states but did not agree that those specifics were the only rights protected under the fourteenth amendment.

The course of the decisions in recent years has tended to obscure the application of the fundamental rights theory. The judicial protection of economic and proprietary liberties—the liberties emphasized in the early substantive rights interpretation of the due process clause—has declined. The Court has said that these liberties are subject to restriction in the reasonable exercise of the states' power to regulate economic matters, and has made it clear that in this area judicial review of the reasonableness of legislation operates at a minimal level.[15] Indeed, Justices Black and Douglas, in writing for the Court in some of the cases, have stated that the Court is not free to inquire at all into the reasonableness of restrictions on economic liberty, since that is an intrusion into the legislative domain in areas where the Constitution imposes no specific restriction.[16] On the other hand, the Court has come to recognize that all of the first amendment freedoms are fundamental and therefore protected against the states under the due process clause of the fourteenth amendment.[17] Likewise, the Court has found in more recent decisions that some of the procedural safeguards embodied in the specifics of the Bill of Rights are fundamental and must therefore be respected by the states. The right to counsel,[18] the freedom from unreasonable search and seizure,[19] the privilege against self-incrimina-

---

15. Day-Brite Lighting, Inc. v. Missouri, 342 U.S. 421 (1952); West Coast Hotel Co. v. Parrish, 300 U.S. 379 (1937); Nebbia v. New York, 291 U.S. 502 (1934).

16. See Mr. Justice Douglas' opinion for the Court in Olsen v. Nebraska *ex rel.* Western Reference & Bond Ass'n, 313 U.S. 236 (1941), and Mr. Justice Black's opinions for the Court in Lincoln Federal Labor Union v. Northwestern Iron & Metal Co., 335 U.S. 525 (1949), and Ferguson v. Skrupa, 372 U.S. 726 (1963). Mr. Justice Harlan concurred in a separate opinion in *Skrupa*, on the ground that the statute there involved bore "a rational relation to a constitutionally permissible objective." *Id.* at 733.

In his opinion in Lincoln Federal Labor Union v. Northwestern Iron & Metal Co., *supra*, Mr. Justice Black said that, beginning with the *Nebbia* case, the Court had steadily rejected the due process philosophy enunciated in the *Adair-Coppage* line of cases, and in so doing had consciously returned closer and closer "to the earlier constitutional principle that states have power to legislate against what are found to be injurious practices in their internal commercial and business affairs, so long as their laws do not run afoul of some specific federal constitutional prohibition, or of some valid federal law." 335 U.S. at 536.

17. Cantwell v. Connecticut, 310 U.S. 296 (1940) (freedom of religion); De Jonge v. Oregon, 299 U.S. 353 (1937) (freedom of assembly); Near v. Minnesota, 283 U.S. 697 (1931) (freedom of press); Gitlow v. New York, 268 U.S. 652 (1925) (freedom of speech).

The freedom from expropriation of property without compensation, guaranteed by the fifth amendment, is also recognized as a fundamental right protected under the fourteenth amendment. See Griggs v. Allegheny County, 369 U.S. 84 (1962); Chicago, B. & Q.R.R. v. Chicago, 166 U.S. 226 (1897). Likewise the prohibition of cruel and unusual punishment, found in the eighth amendment, has been made effective against the states under the fourteenth amendment. Robinson v. California, 370 U.S. 660 (1962).

18. Gideon v. Wainwright, 372 U.S. 335 (1963).

19. Mapp v. Ohio, 367 U.S. 643 (1961).

tion,[20] and the right of confrontation[21] have been extended to the states by virtue of the due process clause. Moreover, the Court has now made it clear that when a right specifically embodied in the Bill of Rights is recognized as fundamental, it has the same full scope and meaning as a restriction on state action as it does in its primary context within the Bill of Rights as a restriction on the federal government.[22] It is in this sense that the first amendment and the provisions of the Bill of Rights specifying the procedural guarantees mentioned above are said to be incorporated into the fourteenth amendment.

Notwithstanding the emphasis in recent years on the protection under the fourteenth amendment of certain specifics of the Bill of Rights, the Court has continued to afford protection in the name of due process against governmental restrictions found to constitute unwarranted or unreasonable interference with rights or liberties not included in the specifics of the first eight amendments. Thus, it has invalidated under the due process clause of the fourteenth amendment a state statute subjecting public employees to arbitrary dismissal[23] and a state regulation arbitrarily restricting admission to the bar.[24] The Court relied on the due process clause of the fifth amendment to invalidate racial segregation in the schools of the District of Columbia.[25] Similarly, in holding invalid the federal restriction on the issuance of passports to Communists, the Court found that the statute was an unduly broad restriction on the right to travel, which was declared to be a fundamental liberty protected under the due process clause of the fifth amendment.[26] In addition, the Court has never overruled cases of earlier vintage such as *Meyer*

---

20. Malloy v. Hogan, 378 U.S. 1 (1964).
21. Pointer v. Texas, 380 U.S. 400 (1965).
22. See Mr. Justice Brennan's opinion for the Court in Malloy v. Hogan, 378 U.S. 1 (1964), and Mr. Justice Goldberg's separate opinion in Pointer v. Texas, *supra* note 21. Mr. Justice Harlan has dissented from this view, taking the position that state criminal procedures are invalid under the due process clause only if they are fundamentally unfair. See his dissenting opinion in Malloy v. Hogan, *supra*, and the concurring opinions by Justices Harlan and Stewart in the *Pointer* case, *supra*. Mr. Justice Harlan likewise makes a distinction between the fundamental freedoms of expression protected against state action under the due process clause and the freedoms stated in the first amendment as a restriction on Congress. See his separate opinion in Roth v. United States, 354 U.S. 476 (1957). To the same effect, see Mr. Justice Jackson's dissenting opinion in Beauharnais v. Illinois, 343 U.S. 250 (1952).
23. Wieman v. Updegraff, 344 U.S. 183 (1952).
24. Schware v. Board of Bar Examiners, 353 U.S. 232 (1957).
25. "Segregation in public education is not reasonably related to any proper governmental objective, and thus it imposes on Negro children of the District of Columbia a burden that constitutes an arbitrary deprivation of their liberty in violation of the Due Process Clause." Bolling v. Sharpe, 347 U.S. 497, 500 (1954).
26. Aptheker v. Secretary of State, 378 U.S. 500 (1964). See also Kent v. Dulles, 357 U.S. 116 (1958).

v. Nebraska,[27] invalidating a Nebraska statute forbidding the use of foreign languages in teaching public school classes, and *Pierce v. Society of Sisters*,[28] invalidating an Oregon statute requiring parents to send their children to public schools. The Nebraska statute was found to be an arbitrary interference with "the calling of modern language teachers, with the opportunities of pupils to acquire knowledge, and with the power of parents to control the education of their own";[29] the Oregon statute was found to be an arbitrary interference with the liberty of parents to direct the upbringing and education of their children. These cases were clearly grounded on the fundamental rights interpretation of the due process clause, and there has been no suggestion in later cases that they have been repudiated.[30]

The decisions in the main line of interpretation of the fourteenth amendment support the following conclusions: (1) The Court has not accepted the thesis that the effect of the fourteenth amendment is to make all of the first eight amendments applicable to the states. (2) The Court has adhered to the idea that the due process clause protects only those rights that are fundamental, and that specifics of the Bill of Rights are absorbed into the fourteenth amendment only because they are regarded as fundamental. (3) The Court has continued to recognize that the fundamental rights protected under the due process clauses of both the fifth and fourteenth amendments may include rights not included in the specifics of the Bill of Rights.

II. Analysis of the *Griswold* Opinions

A. *Introduction: The Poe v. Ullman Dissents*

The opinions in *Griswold* must be examined against the background of this historical development to see what contribution they have made in this troubled area of constitutional interpretation.

---

27. 262 U.S. 390 (1923).

28. 268 U.S. 510 (1925).

29. Meyer v. Nebraska, 262 U.S. 390, 394 (1923).

30. For other earlier cases, see Jacobson v. Massachusetts, 197 U.S. 11 (1905), upholding a compulsory vaccination law, and Buck v. Bell, 274 U.S. 200 (1927), upholding a statute authorizing compulsory sterilization of mental defectives in state institutions. Both cases rested on the assumption that the due process clause afforded protection against arbitrary or unreasonable invasion of bodily integrity. See also Skinner v. Oklahoma, 316 U.S. 535 (1942), holding invalid under the equal protection clause a statute requiring sterilization of certain classes of habitual criminals. Mr. Justice Douglas, who wrote the majority opinion, said that the statute involved one of "the basic civil rights of man." *Id.* at 541.

For other cases resting on the use of the due process clause to protect against unreasonable restriction on personal liberties, see Griswold v. Connecticut, 381 U.S. at 504 n.* (separate opinion of White, J.)

First, however, attention should be called to the dissenting opinions of Justices Douglas and Harlan in the earlier case of *Poe v. Ullman*,[31] in which the Court refused to pass on the constitutionality of the Connecticut birth control law on the ground that such a decision would be premature, since there was no showing that the statute was actually being enforced. In their separate opinions these two Justices, after concluding that the elements of a justiciable case or controversy were present, found the Connecticut ban on the use of contraceptives unconstitutional because of its invasion of the right of privacy of married couples.

In his *Poe* dissent, Mr. Justice Douglas said that although he believed that "due process" as used in the fourteenth amendment included all the protections of the first eight amendments, he did not think it was confined to them.[32] He cited several cases to support his view that the liberty protected by the due process clause includes liberties in addition to those stated in the first eight amendments.[33] Indeed, he suggested that the due process clause could be used as a basis for inquiry concerning the constitutionality of social legislation dealing with business and economic matters, and that while the legislative judgment on these matters is nearly conclusive, it is not beyond judicial inquiry.[34] Apparently Mr. Justice Douglas was ready to use the "liberty" phrase of the due process clause as a source of judicially protected rights and interests, apart from the specifics of the Bill of Rights. He said that "liberty" was a conception that sometimes gained content from either the emanations of the specific guarantees "or from experience with the requirements of a free society."[35] He characterized the right of privacy as emanating "from the totality of the constitutional scheme under which we live."[36] This language obviously bears a close relationship to such language as "fundamental principles of liberty and justice," "ordered liberty," and the other phrases used in the past to define the fundamental rights protected under the due process clause.

Mr. Justice Harlan, dissenting in *Poe*, found the Connecticut statute invalid because it was an unwarranted invasion by the state of the privacy of the marital relationship, which he asserted was protected as a fundamental liberty secured by the fourteenth amendment. His opinion is notable for its review and reasoned defense of

---

31. 367 U.S. 497 (1961).
32. *Id.* at 516.
33. *E.g.*, Kent v. Dulles, 357 U.S. 116 (1958) (right to travel); Meyer v. Nebraska, 262 U.S. 390, 399 (1923) (right to marry, establish a home, and bring up children).
34. Poe v. Ullman, 367 U.S. 497, 518 (1961) (dissenting opinion).
35. *Id.* at 517.
36. *Id.* at 521.

the fundamental rights theory. This dissenting opinion impresses me as not only the ablest and most persuasive opinion that has been written on this subject, but also, because of its careful analysis of the right of marital privacy, the best opinion that has been written on the constitutionality of the Connecticut statute. Mr. Justice Harlan made it clear that he did not rest his decision on the ground that the statute's general policy against the use of contraceptives was an irrational exercise of the police power; his objection was to the method by which the state attempted to enforce this policy insofar as it reached into the privacy of the marital home. Because he regarded this as a particularly sensitive area, he felt that the Court was under a special duty to protect this relationship against arbitrary invasion.

B. *The Opinion of the Court: Mr. Justice Douglas*

We turn now to the *Griswold* opinions. Mr. Justice Douglas' unusually short opinion of the Court combined a curious, puzzling mixture of reasoning with extraordinary freedom in the interpretation of earlier cases. His whole opinion was directed to the end of demonstrating that the right of marital privacy is protected under the Bill of Rights and then carried over as a restriction on the states via the fourteenth amendment. At the outset he seemingly rejected the possibility of invalidating the Connecticut statute on the ground that its policy against the use of contraceptives constituted an unreasonable exercise of the police power and hence a deprivation of liberty without due process of law.[37] Rather, it was the direct operation of the law on the intimate relation of husband and wife, and on their physician's role in one aspect of that relation, which raised the crucial issue. He stated that the Constitution has protected certain rights which are derived from the Bill of Rights, although not expressly named there. He spoke of rights "peripheral" to the specifics named in the first eight amendments and argued that without these peripheral rights the specific rights would be less secure. Thus, he said, the Court has interpreted the first amendment as including such peripheral rights as the right of association.[38] On the basis of this peripheral rights reasoning—and at this point the reader experiences a sense of confusion—he interpreted the *Meyer* and *Pierce* cases to mean that the first amendment forbids a state to "contract the spectrum of available knowledge";[39] he then concluded that part

37. "Overtones of some arguments suggest that *Lochner* v. *New York* . . . should be our guide. But we decline that invitation. . . . We do not sit as a super-legislature to determine the wisdom, need, and propriety of laws that touch economic problems, business affairs, or social conditions." 381 U.S. at 482.

38. See Brotherhood of R.R. Trainmen v. Virginia *ex rel.* Virginia State Bar, 377 U.S. 1 (1964); NAACP v. Button, 371 U.S. 415 (1963).

39. 381 U.S. at 481-82.

of the opinion by saying, "and so we reaffirm the principle of the *Pierce* and *Meyer* cases."[40]

But then Mr. Justice Douglas went on to restate the peripheral rights theory. He interpreted the cases previously cited in support of the notion of peripheral rights to mean that the specific guarantees have penumbras, formed by emanations from those guarantees, that help give them life and substance. At that point he went to the heart of his argument, saying that "zones of privacy" are created by various guarantees: the first amendment, which in its penumbra includes the privacy linked with the freedom of association; the third amendment, which prohibits the quartering of soldiers in any house in time of peace without the consent of the owner; the fourth amendment, which protects against unreasonable search and seizure; and the fifth amendment, which protects against self-incrimination. He also threw in for good measure the ninth amendment, although its relevancy to his argument in showing a zone of privacy is not apparent. He quoted the language of *Boyd v. United States*[41] that the fourth and fifth amendments protect against all governmental invasions of "the sanctity of a man's home and the privacies of life,"[42] and the statement in *Mapp v. Ohio*[43] that the fourth amendment creates "a right to privacy, no less important than any other right carefully and particularly reserved to the people."[44] He said that the Court has had many controversies over the penumbral rights of "privacy and repose," and construed those cases[45] to bear witness that the right of privacy pressing for recognition in *Griswold* was a legitimate one.

Griswold, he continued, "concerns a relationship lying within the zone of privacy created by several fundamental constitutional guarantees. And it concerns a law which, in forbidding the *use* of contraceptives rather than regulating their manufacture or sale, seeks to achieve its goals by means having a maximum destructive impact upon that relationship."[46] Such a law could not stand, because " 'a governmental purpose to control or prevent activities constitutionally subject to state regulation may not be achieved by means which sweep unnecessarily broadly and thereby invade the area of protected freedoms.' "[47]

40. *Id.* at 483.
41. 116 U.S. 616 (1886).
42. *Id.* at 630.
43. 367 U.S. 643 (1961).
44. *Id.* at 656.
45. *E.g.*, Monroe v. Pape, 365 U.S. 167 (1961); Frank v. Maryland, 359 U.S. 360 (1959); Breard v. Alexandria, 341 U.S. 622 (1951).
46. 381 U.S. at 485.
47. *Id.* at 485 (quoting from NAACP v. Alabama, 377 U.S. 288, 307 (1958)).

The opinion concluded with the following paragraph:

> We deal with a right of privacy older than the Bill of Rights
> —older than our political parties, older than our school sys-
> tem. Marriage . . . is an association that promotes a way of life,
> not causes; a harmony in living, not political faiths; a bilateral
> loyalty, not commercial or social projects. Yet it is an association
> for as noble a purpose as any involved in our prior decisions.[48]

Taken as a whole, Mr. Justice Douglas' opinion is ambiguous
and uncertain in its use of the specifics of the Bill of Rights to invalidate the Connecticut statute. Is the right of privacy included
within the penumbra of the marriage association and is this association in turn identifiable, as suggested by the last paragraph of the
opinion, with a general right of association peripheral to the first
amendment freedoms? Or is the intimacy of the marriage relationship included within a general zone of privacy of home and family
derived both from the specifically protected zones of privacy and
the penumbra of privacy emanating from specific rights? Or is it the
theory of the case that the Connecticut statute violated the fundamental rights associated with family and the home, not because the
statute rested on a policy which unreasonably interfered with these
rights but because it employed means which violated a right of
privacy derived from the specifics of the Bill of Rights? Whatever
the interpretation, it is clear that Mr. Justice Douglas worked hard
in his opinion to demonstrate that the decision does not rest in-
dependently on an interpretation of the due process clause, but is
based on implications from those of the first eight amendments
which are made applicable to the states by means of the fourteenth
amendment.

C. *Concurring Opinions*

1. *Mr. Justice Goldberg*

Mr. Justice Goldberg, joined by Mr. Chief Justice Warren and
Mr. Justice Brennan, wrote a separate opinion. Although he said
at the outset that he concurred both in the judgment and the opinion
of the Court, Mr. Justice Goldberg devoted the major part of his
opinion to the elaboration of a separate theory having no necessary
relation to the notion that the right of privacy at issue is an emanation from specifics of the Bill of Rights or embraced within the
penumbra of these rights. While Mr. Justice Goldberg does not
accept the view that due process as used in the fourteenth amendment includes all of the first eight amendments, he does agree that

---

48. *Id.* at 486.

the concept of liberty protects those personal rights that are fundamental, and is not confined to the specific terms of the Bill of Rights.
The major portion of his opinion was devoted to an elaboration of
the fundamental rights theory. He repeated with apparent approval
the Court's statement in *Snyder v. Massachusetts*[49] that the due
process clause protects rights that are "so rooted in the traditions
and conscience of our people as to be ranked as fundamental."[50] To
support the proposition that the liberty protected under the due
process clause includes the right to marry, establish a home, and
bring up children, he referred to the *Meyer* case and to other cases
in which the Court has used the due process clauses of the fifth and
fourteenth amendments to protect fundamental personal liberties.
This part of his opinion is basically a restatement of the classic
fundamental rights theory. What is really novel, however, about
Mr. Justice Goldberg's opinion is that he further supports the
Court's role in protecting fundamental rights other than those stated
in the Constitution by falling back on the ninth amendment.[51] For
him the ninth amendment shows the intent of the Constitution's
authors that fundamental personal rights should not be denied protection simply because they are not specifically listed in the first eight
amendments.

Mr. Justice Goldberg went on to say that the right of privacy is
a fundamental personal right emanating "from the totality of the
constitutional scheme under which we live,"[52] and that the Connecticut statute dealt with a particularly important and sensitive
area of privacy—that of the home and the marital relation. Connecticut had not shown that the law served any "subordinating interest
which is compelling"[53] or that it was "necessary and not merely rationally related, to the accomplishment of a permissible state
policy."[54] At most, the state argued that there was *some* rational
relation between this statute and what was admittedly a legitimate
subject of state concern—the discouragement of extramarital relations. While questioning the rationality of this justification, Mr.
Justice Goldberg said that "in any event it [was] clear that the state

---

49. 291 U.S. 97 (1934).
50. 381 U.S. at 487 (quoting from Snyder v. Massachusetts, 291 U.S. 97, 105 (1934)).
See also *id.* at 493, where in stating the fundamental rights theory he draws upon the
language in Mr. Justice Douglas' dissenting opinion in the *Poe* case, quoted in text
accompanying note 35 *supra*.
51. "The enumeration in the Constitution, of certain rights, shall not be construed
to deny or disparage others retained by the people." U.S. Const. amend. IX.
52. 381 U.S. at 494 (quoting from Poe v. Ullman, 367 U.S. 497, 521 (dissenting
opinion of Douglas, J.)).
53. *Id.* at 497 (quoting from Bates v. City of Little Rock, 361 U.S. 516, 524 (1960)).
54. *Ibid.* (quoting from McLaughlin v. Florida, 379 U.S. 184, 196 (1964)).

interest in safeguarding marital fidelity could be served by a more discriminately tailored statute, which [did] not . . . sweep unnecessarily broadly, reaching far beyond the evil sought to be dealt with and intruding upon the privacy of all married couples."[55]

2. *Mr. Justice Harlan*

Mr. Justice Harlan's concurring opinion very clearly disassociated itself from the Douglas opinion, which Harlan reads as adopting the view that the fourteenth amendment protects only the rights guaranteed by the letter or the penumbra of the Bill of Rights. Just as Mr. Justice Harlan rejects the notion that the effect of the fourteenth amendment is to make the specifics of the Bill of Rights apply to the states, so he also rejects the idea that the fourteenth amendment cannot be used to protect rights that are not stated in the Bill of Rights. He rests his concurrence on the views he stated at length in his dissenting opinion in the *Poe* case, where he found the Connecticut statute invalid as an intrusion upon the intimacies of the marital relation that come within the protection accorded to the home.

3. *Mr. Justice White*

Mr. Justice White in his separate concurring opinion also clearly disassociated himself from the notion implicit in the majority opinion that only those rights embraced within the letter or the penumbra of the Bill of Rights are protected under the fourteenth amendment. He fell back upon the general theory that the fourteenth amendment protects against arbitrary or capricious denial of liberty and that the liberty thus protected includes the right "to marry, establish a home and bring up children"[56] and "the liberty . . . to direct the upbringing and education of children,"[57] and that these are among the "basic civil rights of man."[58] He also spoke of the right "to be free of regulation of the intimacies of the marriage relationship."[59] Thus, any statute forbidding the use of birth control devices by married persons, prohibiting doctors from giving advice to married persons on proper and effective methods of birth control, and having the clear effect of denying to disadvantaged citizens of the state access to medical assistance and up-to-date information with respect to methods of birth control, bears a substantial burden of justification when attacked under the fourteenth amendment. Con-

---

55. *Id.* at 497-98.
56. *Id.* at 502 (quoting from Meyer v. Nebraska, 262, 390, 399 (1923)).
57. *Ibid.* (quoting from Pierce v. Society of Sisters, 268 U.S. 510, 534-35 (1925)).
58. *Ibid.* (quoting from Skinner v. Oklahoma, 316 U.S. 535, 541 (1942)).
59. *Id.* at 503.

ceding that the state's policy against all forms of promiscuous or illicit sexual relationships is a permissible legislative goal, Mr. Justice White then proceeded to demonstrate that this particular restriction on the use of contraceptive devices by married couples could not be justified by reference to that legitimate public policy. The distinctive feature of Mr. Justice White's opinion, apart from the fact that it is a clear articulation of the substantive rights interpretation of due process, is the care with which he examines the Connecticut law in determining whether any rational consideration appropriate to matters of public concern justifies the restriction.

D. *Dissenting Opinions*

1. *Mr. Justice Black*

For those acquainted with Mr. Justice Black's dissenting opinion in the *Adamson* case, his dissent in *Griswold* comes as no surprise, since in his *Adamson* dissent he had already taken the position that the fourteenth amendment makes the Bill of Rights applicable to the states and that there is no basis for a judicial formulation of fundamental rights other than those embraced by the specifics of the first eight amendments. His dissent in large part reaffirms the basic idea set forth in his *Adamson* opinion—that it is the business of the Court to protect the specific rights guaranteed in the Constitution but not to pass judgment on the reasonableness of state legislative enactments alleged to impair other fundamental rights that have their source in a natural-law type of thinking. He therefore basically disagrees with the theory expressed by Justices Harlan and White in their concurring opinions. Likewise, he cannot accept the view stated by Mr. Justice Goldberg that the ninth amendment is a basis for judicial assertion of new fundamental rights, since, as he sees it, this is simply another way of stating the discredited natural rights philosophy. Moreover, he rejects the theory stated in Mr. Justice Douglas' opinion that the right of privacy involved in *Griswold* is embraced within the penumbra of rights specified in the Bill of Rights; he feels that it is much too broad a generalization to say that the specifics of the Bill of Rights create a general right of privacy of the kind relied upon by the Court.

2. *Mr. Justice Stewart*

Mr. Justice Stewart dissented on essentially the same grounds.[60] He agreed with Mr. Justice Black that the use of the ninth amend-

---

60. Mr. Justice Stewart's dissenting opinion in *Griswold* is the first clear-cut statement by him rejecting the formulation in the name of the due process clause of a

ment added nothing to the case so far as the Court's power to protect rights not specifically mentioned in the Bill of Rights is concerned, since the purpose of both the ninth and tenth amendments was to make clear that the federal government was to be a government of express, limited powers and that all rights and powers not delegated to it were retained by the people. Indeed, in his view, to say that the ninth amendment, intended as a restriction on the federal government, has anything to do with this case, involving the validity of a state statute, "is to turn somersaults with history."[61]

III. The Contribution of *Griswold* to General Constitutional Theory

In appraising the significance of *Griswold* we must distinguish between the immediate impact of the case and its larger significance in terms of general constitutional theory. *Griswold* holds no more than that a statute prohibiting the use of contraceptives by married couples is invalid as an invasion of a right of marital privacy protected against the states under the fourteenth amendment. The case does not mean that a state may not prohibit the manufacture and sale of contraceptives; still less does it suggest any questioning of the validity of laws dealing with illicit sexual relations. Two important types of right are stressed: the rights associated with marriage, family, and the home, and a right of privacy incident to constitutionally protected activities and relations. Family and marital rights have assumed a new constitutional significance, and fresh vitality has been given to the *Meyer* and *Pierce* decisions. Furthermore, recognition of the right of privacy may well be an opening wedge for extension of that right in new directions.

The larger significance of the case, however, is the contribution, if any, that it makes to general constitutional theory respecting fundamental rights, the relationship of these rights to the specifics of the Bill of Rights, and the standard to be employed by the Court in passing on the constitutionality of legislation allegedly impinging on fundamental rights.

A. *Application of the Bill of Rights Guarantees to the States*

Griswold does not bear directly on the question whether the effect of the fourteenth amendment is to make all the specifics of

---

theory of fundamental substantive rights not identifiable with the specifics of the first eight amendments. Compare his position, as expressed in his concurring opinion in Pointer v. Texas, 380 U.S. 400 (1965), that the due process clause assures a fundamental right to procedural fairness, and his reference in his opinion in *Griswold*, 381 U.S. at 528, to the use of the due process clause for that purpose.

61. 381 U.S. at 529.

the Bill of Rights apply to the states, but it seems clear that Justices Black and Douglas have gained no new converts to their position on this issue. Indeed, Mr. Justice Goldberg, in his concurring opinion joined by Mr. Chief Justice Warren and Mr. Justice Brennan, expressly said that he has not accepted that view, although he does agree that the fourteenth amendment does make applicable to the states the specifics which are fundamental. Mr. Justice Harlan has always made it abundantly clear that he totally rejects the incorporation theory in all of its aspects. Justices Clark, Stewart, and White have never identified themselves with the Black-Douglas thesis, and nothing in the separate opinions by Justices White and Stewart in *Griswold* would suggest an acceptance of that thesis. At most, then, it may be said that a majority of the Justices are ready to find that specifics of the Bill of Rights apply to the states only when those specifics are identified as fundamental rights. It is worth emphasizing that a majority could not have been mustered in *Griswold* to hold the statute invalid except for the concurrence of those Justices who found the statute invalid as an invasion of a right which they characterized as "fundamental."

B. *Fourteenth Amendment Protection of Rights Not Specified in the Bill of Rights*

The most immediate impact of the *Griswold* decision is on the concomitant question whether rights not specified in the Bill of Rights are protected under the due process clause of the fourteenth amendment. The decision is ambiguous in this respect. According to one view expressed in the case and supported by five of the Justices,[62] the right of privacy on which the case hangs is embraced within the penumbra or periphery of specifics guaranteed in the first eight amendments. On the other hand, it is also clear that the idea that the right of privacy is a fundamental right quite apart from the specifics of the Bill of Rights also receives the support of a majority of the Justices. Certainly Justices Harlan and White support this view, and I interpret Mr. Justice Goldberg's opinion to the same effect, although the fundamental rights thinking in his opinion is bolstered by an appeal to the ninth amendment. *Griswold* can thus be interpreted as a reaffirmation by a majority of the Court of the

---

62. This is the view expressed in the opinion of the Court written by Mr. Justice Douglas. Mr. Justice Clark concurred in this sub silentio, since he did not write a separate opinion. Mr. Justice Goldberg, joined by Justices Warren and Brennan, concurred in the Douglas opinion, although he also found an independent basis for the result in the fundamental rights theory.

fundamental rights theory—both in the sense that only fundamental rights derived from the Bill of Rights are incorporated into the fourteenth amendment and in the sense that the due process clause is a source of rights apart from the specifics of the Bill of Rights.

C. *The Standard To Be Employed in Evaluating State Legislation*

One of the more important aspects of the case is the strict standard employed by the Court in determining whether the Connecticut statute forbidding the use of contraceptives was constitutional as applied to married couples. It was not enough for the state to point to what it regarded as some rational considerations to support the restriction on married couples as a means of enforcing a general policy directed against promiscuous or extramarital sexual relations. The opinion by Mr. Justice Douglas applied the familiar idea of the overbroad statute: a legitimate governmental policy cannot be achieved by means which are so unnecessarily broad that they invade areas of protected freedom. Mr. Justice Goldberg's opinion stressed the idea that when a statute impairs fundamental personal liberties, the state must show that it is justified by a compelling public interest, and the law must be carefully tailored so as not to reach beyond the evil sought to be dealt with by intruding upon an important constitutional interest. In his dissent in *Poe*, Mr. Justice Harlan said that when a statute abridges fundamental liberties, a closer scrutiny is required than that indicated by the rationality test; he found nothing that even remotely justified the obnoxiously intrusive means employed by Connecticut to effectuate a policy expressing the state's concern for its citizens' moral welfare. He pointed to the "utter novelty" of the Connecticut statute's ban on the use of contraceptives by married couples.[63] Mr. Justice White, in his concurring opinion in *Griswold,* stressed the point that a state cannot enter the realm of family life "without substantial justification,"[64] and devoted a major part of his opinion to showing that no substantial justification was put forth to justify the sweeping scope of the statute and its telling effect on the freedom of married persons.

It is thus evident that the several members of the Court feel that an exacting judicial scrutiny, like that employed in cases involving first amendment freedoms, is required when legislation impinges upon the realm of the family life and marital relationship.

---

63. Poe v. Ullman, 367 U.S. 497, 554 (1961).
64. 381 U.S. at 502.

IV. Some Comments and Observations

A. *No Major Change in Constitutional Theory*

Insofar as the result in *Griswold* rests on the fundamental rights interpretation of the due process clause of the fourteenth amendment, and as I interpret the opinions five Justices can be counted in support of this theory, the case states no new theory and is consistent with the main line of development under the substantive rights interpretation of the liberty protected by the due process clause. It also supports the statement made earlier that the Court has never repudiated the fundamental rights theory. Furthermore, the result is not at all inconsistent with the cases that have reduced economic liberty to a minimum of judicial protection, whether by denying that liberty of contract is a constitutionally protected right or by holding that it is subject to legislation that meets the test of rationality. The freedom of a legislature to determine economic policy in the public interest stands on a quite different level from its freedom to determine social policy by means that intrude upon personal liberty and essentially private conduct. It is fair to suppose that, notwithstanding statements to the contrary in some opinions, the Court will continue to recognize some basis for judicial protection of economic and proprietary liberties. The essential point is that restrictions on economic liberty are subject to a less exacting judicial scrutiny, with greater deference being shown to the legislative judgment. Here the simple rationality test applies,[65] but when legislation impinges upon fundamental non-economic liberties of an essentially personal character, as in *Griswold*, a more exacting judicial test is applied. There is nothing new about the idea that the Court sees a hierarchy of values protected under the Constitution and that the degree of judicial scrutiny and protection varies in direct proportion to the importance of the right. The frequently voiced notion that first amendment freedoms are "preferred" is an expression of this idea.[66] Similarly, in the interpretation of the equal protection clause the Court has made it clear that it is ready to depart from the rationality test in examining the constitutionality of legislative classification when the classification either rests on a factor that the Court regards as impermissible in view of our whole constitutional tradition or serves the purpose of impairing important personal interests.[67]

---

65. See Griswold v. Connecticut, 381 U.S. 479, 503 (1965) (concurring opinion of White, J.); Poe v. Ullman, 367 U.S. 497, 518 (1961) (dissenting opinion of Douglas, J.).

66. See McKay, *The Preference for Freedom*, 34 N.Y.U.L. Rev. 1182 (1959).

67. See McLaughlin v. Florida, 379 U.S. 184 (1965) (White, J.), rejecting the rationality test when legislation is based on a racial classification; Skinner v. Oklahoma, 316

B. *Criticism of Mr. Justice Douglas' Opinion*

The opinion by Mr. Justice Douglas appears to me to be a labored attempt to identify the right of marital privacy with the specifics of the Bill of Rights. It says, when we penetrate the special vocabulary (peripheral rights, penumbras formed by emanations from specific rights, zones of privacy), that the right of marital privacy is implied from an aggregate of specifics. I have no difficulty with such a theory of implied rights. For example, the right to associate for the purpose of expressing views on political, economic, and social matters seems fairly to be implied from the first amendment. It is another thing, however, to suggest that because marriage is a form of association it comes within the protection afforded freedom of association. The Bill of Rights does in various specifics recognize zones of privacy in protecting persons, their homes, and even their political views from intrusion by government. Again, however, it is quite another thing to say that a general right of marital privacy can be distilled from these specifics.[68] It is not stretching things to say that the sanctity of the home protected against unreasonable searches and seizures implies a privacy of family life, as Mr. Justice Harlan pointed out in his illuminating dissent in *Poe*. But it protects this privacy against unreasonable intrusions by public officers; it is another thing to hold unconstitutional a law which has the effect of intruding into this privacy by subjecting marital intimacies to criminal sanctions and which could therefore be authority for a search and seizure to determine whether the statute is being violated. Insofar as the Court assumes to invalidate legislation by converting a freedom from unreasonable police searches into a fundamental substantive right restricting legislative action in formulating social policy, it is engaging in that expansive use of the judicial power to formulate conceptions of fundamental rights as a limitation on legislative invasion which has characterized the judicial role under the due process clause.

The point of the foregoing discussion is that a theory of rights implied from the specifics of the Bill of Rights can be pushed to the point where the distinction between such "implied" rights and the formulation of "fundamental" rights in the interpretation of the due process clause is wholly verbal and without substance. The question that may be raised about all this is whether the Court,

---

U.S. 535 (1942), holding invalid a classification used in a statute requiring the sterilization of habitual criminals; Reynolds v. Sims, 377 U.S. 533 (1964), holding invalid a state legislative apportionment system because of its discriminatory impact on the right to vote.

68. 381 U.S. 479, 508-09 (dissenting opinion of Black, J.).

through the peripheral-emanations-penumbra process of interpretation, is really finding a more objective and more secure basis for the new right it has recognized than is found in the fundamental rights interpretation of the due process clause. Indeed, in order to command the support of a majority of the Court, it is still essential to find that the right embraced within penumbras of the specifics of the Bill of Rights is a fundamental right; judicial subjectivity thus still plays a crucial part in the final decision.

The accordion-like qualities of the emanations-and-penumbra theory, and the ease with which it can be used in the same broad way in which the fundamental rights theory has been used, become evident when one considers its application to areas where the Court in recent years has limited the sphere of constitutional protection. The point is made that since liberty of contract is not mentioned in the Constitution, it should not be a constitutionally protected right. Yet, since the body of the Constitution protects against the impairment of the obligations of contracts, it does not require a far-fetched application of the emanations-and-penumbra theory to suggest that implicit in the contracts clause (or at least radiating from it) is a constitutional right to enter into contracts. Likewise, it may be suggested that since the fifth amendment protects property against expropriation without compensation, there is surely a penumbra of rights emanating from this which would include the right to acquire and enjoy the use of property without arbitrary interference by the government. I am not suggesting that the Court will arrive at these results through the application of the peripheral-emanations-penumbra idea. The only point I wish to make is that in extending the specifics to the periphery, and in finding rights derived from the total scheme of the Bill of Rights, the Court is applying essentially the same process as that used in the fundamental rights approach, but dignifying it with a different name and thereby creating the illusion of greater objectivity.

As was made clear in the concurring opinions, the past decisions of the Court, notably the *Meyer* and *Pierce* cases, offered an immediate opening for finding that marital privacy, as a facet of the freedom of family life, was a fundamental right. Yet Mr. Justice Douglas, steadfastly adhering to the objective of finding the protected right embraced within the specifics of the first eight amendments, rejected this opening. While declaring that the Court reaffirmed the principles of these two cases, he interpreted them as showing that the first and fourteenth amendments forbid a state to contract the spectrum of learning—an interpretation that would have been astonishing to Mr. Justice McReynolds, who wrote the opinion in these cases, which rested squarely on the fundamental rights interpretation of the due process clause.

It appears also that Mr. Justice Douglas, in his *Griswold* opinion, retreated from his dissenting opinion in *Poe*, where he indicated that the Court should invalidate, in the name of the due process clause, legislation that impinged on an interest "implicit in a free society." His reason for abandoning this idea in *Griswold* is perhaps to be found in the responsibility he faced for writing an opinion for the Court that would avoid the inevitable division flowing from a straightforward substantive rights interpretation of the due process clause. But his effort, if it can be explained on this basis, was not a richly rewarding one in view of the divisions within the Court and the separate concurring opinions.

C. *The Ninth Amendment*

Mr. Justice Goldberg's use of the ninth amendment is an interesting tour de force, but I fail to see how it adds in any substantial way to the argument respecting the fundamental rights theory. For years the Court followed the theory without finding it necessary to fall back on the ninth amendment, which was certainly designed as a limitation on the federal government. Perhaps the ninth amendment argument gives some satisfaction to Justices who have a sense of uneasiness about going outside the Constitution in protecting certain kinds of rights and helps to support further the illusion of objectivity. Even if one were to concede that the use of the ninth amendment negated the Black-Stewart hypothesis, however, it is apparent that the basic problems in the use of the fundamental rights theory still remain: what rights are fundamental and to what limitations are they subject? One may conclude that the ninth amendment adds a nice ornament to the argument, but that is about all. On the other hand, the rejections by Justices Black and Stewart of the ninth amendment argument are not very persuasive either. Their point of emphasis is that the ninth and tenth amendments were intended to make it clear that the federal government is one of restricted powers. This may be conceded, yet the ninth amendment would still support the position taken by Mr. Justice Goldberg that the first eight amendments were not deemed exhaustive of the rights enjoyed by the people. The weakest part, however, of the Black-Stewart argument based on the ninth amendment is that the whole history of the interpretation of the fourteenth amendment has been a story of the forging of new limitations on the states. Particularly at the hands of Mr. Justice Black, it has been a process of making applicable to the states the specifics of the first eight amendments. By equal force of reasoning, the ninth amendment should be incorporated into the fourteenth. If it is a "somersault of history" to use the ninth amendment as a weapon of interpretation in order to restrict a state's legislative power, it is certainly no greater somersault of history than that involved in finding that the states are subject to the establishment-of-religion clause of the first amendment, when it is clear that historically the principal purpose of that clause was to prohibit Congress from interfering with state establishments.[69]

D. *Mr. Justice Black's Thesis*

In his dissenting opinion Mr. Justice Black reaffirmed and enlarged upon the basic view expressed in his dissent in *Adamson* that the Court has no business invalidating state legislation that does not violate the specifics of the Bill of Rights or other specifics found in the Constitution. The whole fundamental rights theory is anathema to him as an expression of judicial subjectivity and of natural rights philosophy. Yet his proposed application to the states of all the specifics of the Bill of Rights is in itself an extraordinary assertion of judicial power, unsupported by the text or history of the fourteenth amendment.[70] Moreover, Black's thesis runs into difficulties when account is taken both of the ninth amendment, which according to his logic should also be made applicable to the states, and of the due process clause of the fifth amendment, both of which furnish means for invalidating governmental action on grounds other than those stated in the specifics of the Bill of Rights. An even more basic consideration, however, is that some of the so-called specifics of the Bill of Rights are not so very specific; they admit of a very large element of judicial subjectivity and discretion in their application, as evidenced by Mr. Justice Douglas' use of peripheries, emanations, and penumbras in his *Griswold* opinion. It happens that Mr. Justice Black cannot subscribe to an expansive use of the specifics in this particular case. Yet it will be recalled that it was Mr. Justice Black who wrote the opinion of the Court in *Brotherhood of Railway Trainmen v. Virginia ex rel. Virginia State Bar*,[71] in which the Court protected, as an associational right under the first amendment, the right of a railway union to assist the prosecution of claims by injured railroad workers through the giving of advice on their rights

---

69. See School Dist. v. Schempp, 374 U.S. 203, 309 (1963) (dissenting opinion of Stewart, J.).

70. See Fairman, *Does the Fourteenth Amendment Incorporate the Bill of Rights? The Original Understanding*, 2 STAN. L. REV. 5 (1949).

71. 377 U.S. 1 (1964).

and the channeling of legal employment to particular lawyers. This is certainly a more extensive and more distinctively marginal use of the first amendment than the use of the specifics to protect the right of privacy in the *Griswold* case.[72] To exclude the privacy of marital association from protection under the Bill of Rights, while using the first amendment as an umbrella for the kind of associational right protected in the *Brotherhood* case, appears to be a case of straining at gnats while swallowing a camel. Moreover, as was suggested by Mr. Justice Harlan in his concurring opinion in *Griswold*, the breadth of the interpretation of the equal protection clause in *Reynolds v. Sims*[73] and of Article I in *Wesberry v. Sanders*,[74] whereby the Court used those provisions as vehicles for invalidating legislative apportionment systems, is a much more audacious and far-reaching judicial interference with the state legislative process, sanctioned neither by history nor by the specifics of the Constitution, than the comparatively innocuous use of judicial power in *Griswold* to invalidate a law which was found on the statute books of a single state and which in most respects was not being enforced. Compared with the use of judicial power in the apportionment cases, *Griswold* is but a tempest in a teapot in its use of judicial power to invalidate a statute impinging on the right of privacy. The equal protection clause is as much an invitation to judicial formulation of policy as the due process clause. In his dissent in *Griswold*, Mr. Justice Black protested against the idea that it is the Court's duty to keep the Constitution in tune with the times and quoted with approval the late Judge Learned Hand's statement that he would find it most irksome "to be ruled by a bevy of Platonic Guardians."[75] Mr. Justice Harlan applauded these sentiments and suggested that the Court would have been well advised to heed this advice when dealing with the apportionment issue.

---

72. See also Robinson v. California, 370 U.S. 660 (1962), where the Court made a curious use of the "cruel and unusual punishment" limitation in invalidating a state statute which, as construed, made it a crime to be a drug addict. This is another instance where the Court, as an alternative to a straightforward application of the familiar idea that the due process clause states an independent substantive limitation on the arbitrary exercise of governmental power, achieved the same result by resorting to a strained interpretation of a Bill of Rights specific in giving content to the due process limitation. See the concurring opinion by Mr. Justice Harlan, and the following language from Mr. Justice White's dissenting opinion: "Finally, I deem this application of 'cruel and unusual punishment' so novel that I suspect the Court was hard put to find a way to ascribe to the Framers of the Constitution the result reached today rather than to its own notions of ordered liberty. If this case involved economic regulation, the present Court's allergy to substantive due process would surely save the statute and prevent the Court from imposing its own philosophical predilections upon state legislatures or Congress." 370 U.S. at 689.
73. 377 U.S. 533 (1964).
74. 376 U.S. 1 (1964).
75. 381 U.S. at 526 (quoting from HAND, THE BILL OF RIGHTS 73 (1958)).

Justices Black and Stewart interpret the Court's recent decisions as a repudiation of fundamental rights thinking. Thus Mr. Justice Black referred to *Griswold* as a retreat from *Ferguson v. Skrupa*,[76] in which he had said that the Court had long since discarded the idea that due process authorizes courts to hold laws unconstitutional when they believe the legislature has acted unwisely. They view recent cases finding legislation invalid under the due process clause as meaning only that the Court uses this clause to enforce procedural fairness, to condemn vague criminal legislation, and to invalidate legislation that abridges the specifics of the Bill of Rights.[77] But surely a case like *Aptheker v. Secretary of State*,[78] holding the denial of passports to Communists invalid under the due process clause as an over-broad restriction on the right to travel protected under the due process clause, is an affirmation of the fundamental rights interpretation of due process. Mr. Justice Black asserted in *Griswold* that if *Aptheker* "was written or intended to bring about the abrupt and drastic reversal in the course of constitutional adjudication which is now attributed to it, the change was certainly made in a very quiet and unprovocative manner, without any attempt to justify it."[79] But one may ask in turn whether all of the Justices who concurred in the *Skrupa* opinion understood that they were overruling sub silentio earlier cases like *Meyer* and *Pierce*. As *Griswold* has made clear, the notion of substantive due process shows a remarkable vitality despite Mr. Justice Black's several efforts to lay it to rest and to pronounce a fitting requiem.

As Justices Black and Stewart so well pointed out, there is always the danger that the Court, in employing the fundamental rights theory, will substitute its judgment for that of the legislature in determining what is wise economic or social policy. This risk, however, is inherent in the system of judicial review and occurs whenever the Court invalidates a legislative act, whether in the name of due process or equal protection, in the name of the broad specifics of the Bill of Rights, or in the name of the peripheral rights embraced in the penumbra of the specifics, and regardless of whether the Court employs a technique of balancing interests or uses a standard of reasonableness, or employs a more exacting judicial scrutiny as in the instant case. The basic problem is not whether a court in exercising the power of judicial review may pass judgment on legislative

76. 372 U.S. 726 (1963).
77. See Griswold v. Connecticut, 381 U.S. at 517 n.10 (dissenting opinion of Black, J.); *id.* at 528, 530 n.7 (dissenting opinion of Stewart, J.). One very interesting aspect of *Griswold* is the wide differences among the Justices in interpreting prior cases.
78. 378 U.S. 500 (1964).
79. 381 U.S. at 517 n.10.

acts, but rather how wisely it exercises this power in identifying, appraising, and weighing the competing interests. The Court is always faced with the task of defining the right and determining the standard to be employed in passing on the constitutionality of legislation impinging on the right. These are two distinctive aspects of the judicial function in these cases. To refuse to recognize a right claimed to be basic to our constitutional order for fear that the Court, in exercising its power to protect that right, will employ a standard whereby it usurps the legislative function in determining basic social policy, obscures analysis of the Court's role and denies the Court's resourcefulness in employing standards appropriate to the particular case. It is worth emphasizing here that the members of the Court who found the Connecticut statute invalid as applied to invade the realm of marital rights did not purport to pass judgment on the wisdom or reasonableness of the general moral policy expressed in the legislation.

E. *Conclusion*

Griswold v. Connecticut is a reaffirmation of a power long exercised by the Court in protecting fundamental rights. It required no judicial roving at large to reach the conclusion that the freedom of the marital relationship is a part of the bundle of rights associated with home, family, and marriage—rights supported by precedent, history, and common understanding. For a court to find that these rights are fundamental, whether because they are deeply written in the tradition and conscience of our people, are part of the concept of ordered liberty, are implicit in the notion of a free society, or emanate from the totality of the constitutional order, involves no immodest or startling exercise of judicial power. The decision operates within a narrow sphere. In exercising its power in *Griswold* to protect a fundamental personal liberty, the Court, far from advancing to a new milepost on the high road to judicial supremacy, was treading a worn and familiar path.

THE RIGHT OF PRIVACY: EMANATIONS AND INTIMATIONS

Robert B. McKay*

I. INTRODUCTION

A. Background: The Legacy of Brandeis

WHEN Louis Brandeis and Samuel Warren wrote in 1890 of "The Right to Privacy,"[1] they sought a means of protecting against unwelcome newspaper attention to social activities in the Warren household.[2] Addressing their argument to the private law of torts, they presumably did not anticipate constitutional protection for other rights under the claim of privacy. Nevertheless, seventy-five years later that concept, now called the "right *of* privacy," was used by the Supreme Court of the United States in *Griswold v. Connecticut*[3] to describe a constitutional right. Some members of the Court said the new right was within the "penumbra" formed by "emanations" from specific guarantees in the Bill of Rights, while others emphasized that it was an always present, but previously undiscovered, "right of the people" preserved in the almost forgotten ninth amendment.[4]

It is ironic that the seventy-five-year-old right of privacy (against tort), although introduced under distinguished sponsorship and widely acclaimed as a forward step in the development of the law, has not yet been clearly defined or even generally acknowledged. William Prosser has described the right of privacy as a protection against "not one tort, but a complex of four."[5] There has been some dissent from that view,[6] and there is no general consensus as to the exact boundaries of the tort. The right of privacy against tort (or against four torts) moved with hesitant steps toward general recognition; in contrast, the constitutional right of privacy, arising out of rather different considerations, apparently became at once fully mature upon first articulation by the Supreme Court in *Griswold*.

---

* Associate Dean and Professor of Law, New York University.—Ed.
1. Warren & Brandeis, *The Right to Privacy*, 4 HARV. L. REV. 193 (1890).
2. See MASON, BRANDEIS—A FREE MAN'S LIFE 70 (1946).
3. Griswold v. Connecticut, 381 U.S. 479 (1965).
4. Even the literature on the ninth amendment is not extensive. See PATTERSON, THE FORGOTTEN NINTH AMENDMENT (1955); Kelsey, *The Ninth Amendment of the Federal Constitution*, 11 IND. L.J. 309 (1936); Redlich, *Are There "Certain Rights . . . Retained by the People"?*, 37 N.Y.U.L. REV. 787 (1962); Rogge, *Unenumerated Rights*, 47 CALIF. L. REV. 787 (1959).
5. Prosser, *Privacy*, 48 CALIF. L. REV. 383, 389 (1960).
6. Bloustein, *Privacy as an Aspect of Human Dignity—An Answer to Dean Prosser*, 39 N.Y.U.L. REV. 962 (1964).

A further irony is the fact that the device that launched the constitutional right of privacy was the humble contraceptive, whose very
existence was little recognized in the polite society whose privacy
Brandeis and Warren sought to protect, but which by 1965 had
become the subject of public hearings in Congress and in many
state capitols, as well as the subject of a feature story with full-color
illustrations in a widely circulated magazine.[7]

One wonders what Mr. Brandeis, as he was in 1890, or Mr.
Justice Brandeis, as he was from 1916 to 1939, would have thought
of these developments. Whatever may have been his original view
of the matter, certainly Brandeis came ultimately to regard the
right of privacy as a concept with more than one facet; one may
speculate that he may have recognized that it was capable of still
further growth. In 1928, long after the 1890 article, Brandeis wrote
his celebrated dissent in *Olmstead v. United States*,[8] in which he
objected strongly to the majority ruling that messages passed along
telephone wires are not within the fourth amendment's protection
against unreasonable searches and seizures. Although he surely did
not then have in mind the specific problem which would be raised
in 1965 in the *Griswold* case, his words had a prophetic quality.
Reminding the Court that clauses in the Constitution have been
broadly interpreted to cover activities and objects "of which the
Fathers could not have dreamed," he warned:

> Clauses guaranteeing to the individual protection against specific
> abuses of power, must have a similar capacity of adaptation to a
> changing world. . . . The progress of science in furnishing the
> Government with means of espionage is not likely to stop with
> wire-tapping. Ways may some day be developed by which the
> Government, without removing papers from secret drawers,
> can reproduce them in court, and by which it will be enabled to
> expose to a jury the most intimate occurrences of the home. . . .
> Can it be that the Constitution affords no protection against such
> invasions of individual security?[9]

Brandeis described "the right to be let alone," the expressive
phrase first used by Judge Cooley,[10] as "the most comprehensive of
rights and the right most valued by civilized men."[11] In emphasizing
the urgent necessity of protecting against "every unjustifiable intru-

---

7. Life, Sept. 10, 1965, p. 59.
8. 277 U.S. 438 (1928).
9. *Id.* at 472, 474.
10. COOLEY, TORTS 29 (2d ed. 1888). See also Griswold, *The Right To Be Let Alone*,
55 NW. U.L. REV. 216 (1960).
11. Olmstead v. United States, 277 U.S. 438, 478 (1928).

sion by the Government upon the privacy of the individual,"[12] Mr. Justice Brandeis borrowed extensively from what Mr. Brandeis had written thirty-eight years earlier.[13]

B. *Griswold v. Connecticut: An Anticlimax and a New Point of Departure*

Despite much off-Court criticism of the majority ruling in *Olmstead* and some expressions of dissatisfaction within the Court, it remains true in 1965, as in 1928, that the only restrictions on wiretapping depend on statute, not on constitutional inhibition. However, the creation of the new right of marital privacy in the home by-passed altogether the constitutional difficulties of the *Olmstead* rationale. Instead, the new right was compounded in some undefined way of the first, third, fourth, fifth, and ninth amendments.

The decision in *Griswold v. Connecticut* answered one question, but perhaps only one. The Court held that the Connecticut statute forbidding the use of contraceptives unconstitutionally invaded the right of marital privacy. By 1965 the ruling on that narrow question was almost anticlimatic. Twice before, in 1943[14] and 1961,[15] the same issue had been presented to the Court, but both cases had been dismissed for lack of standing or ripeness. When the Court finally decided the substantive issue, few remained to defend the statute. The Roman Catholic Church, for instance, which presumably had supported the retention of the Connecticut ban on the use of contraceptives, seemed reconciled to the invalidation of the statute in *Griswold*.[16]

To conclude that there was general satisfaction with the result in *Griswold* is not, however, to suggest that there was general agreement as to the soundness of the constitutional grounds on which the decision was based. Nor should it be thought that those who applauded the result were in accord as to the future significance of the holding. In order to understand why the case raised more questions than it answered, it is necessary first to summarize briefly the various opinions in the case. It will then be possible to sort out some of the possible future "emanations" from a decision that was itself said to be grounded on "emanations" from the Bill of Rights.

---

12. *Ibid.*

13. Edward J. Bloustein noted the nearly verbatim identity of several passages in the 1890 article and the 1928 dissent and concluded that "the underlying conceptual scheme is identical." Bloustein, *supra* note 6, at 976.

14. Tileston v. Ullman, 318 U.S. 44 (1943).

15. Poe v. Ullman, 367 U.S. 497 (1961).

16. See text accompanying notes 102-11 *infra*.

C. *The Griswold Opinions*

Mr. Justice Douglas, writing the opinion of the Court, concluded that "specific guarantees in the Bill of Rights have penumbras, formed by emanations from those guarantees that help give them life and substance."[17] Itemizing, he found that "the First Amendment has a penumbra where privacy is protected from governmental intrusion."[18] He also found facets of privacy in the third amendment's prohibition against the quartering of soldiers "in any house" in time of peace without the consent of the owner; in the fourth amendment's guarantee against unreasonable searches and seizures; in the fifth amendment's privilege against self-incrimination; and in the ninth amendment's reservation of additional, unspecified rights "retained by the people."[19]

Mr. Justice Goldberg, writing for himself, Mr. Chief Justice Warren, and Mr. Justice Brennan, joined in Mr. Justice Douglas' opinion and conclusion that "Connecticut's birth-control law unconstitutionally intrudes upon the right of marital privacy. . . ."[20] His concurring opinion was written "to emphasize the relevance of [the ninth amendment] . . . to the Court's holding."[21]

The ninth amendment, which had almost no judicial interpretation between 1791 and 1965, is at best cryptic: "The enumeration in the Constitution, of certain rights, shall not be construed to deny or disparage others retained by the people." In those words Mr. Justice Goldberg found the constitutional haven he sought for the cherished right to be let alone, at least for the limited purpose of protecting the "private realm of family life."[22] Although he recognized that the Constitution does not expressly mention the right of marital privacy, he nonetheless could not "believe that it offers these fundamental rights no protection. . . . Rather, as the Ninth Amendment expressly recognizes, there are fundamental personal rights such as this one, which are protected from abridgment by the Government though not specifically mentioned in the Constitution."[23] Finally, he contended that where, as in *Griswold*, "fundamental personal liberties are involved, they may not be abridged by the States simply on a

---

17. 381 U.S. at 484.
18. *Id.* at 483.
19. *Id.* at 484.
20. *Id.* at 486.
21. *Id.* at 487.
22. *Id.* at 495, quoting from Prince v. Massachusetts, 321 U.S. 158, 166 (1944). See also Meyer v. Nebraska, 262 U.S. 390, 399 (1923); Pierce v. Society of Sisters, 268 U.S. 510 (1925).
23. 381 U.S. at 495-96.

showing that a regulatory statute has some rational relationship to the effectuation of a proper state purpose."[24]

Justices Harlan and White concurred in the result, but argued that the statute should be held invalid as a violation of the due process clause of the fourteenth amendment, apart from any meaning derived from the Bill of Rights.[25] Their views are more fully discussed in part II below.

In dissent, Mr. Justice Black (joined by Mr. Justice Stewart) objected principally to the Goldberg opinion. Finding no protection for the right of privacy in any provision of the Constitution, Mr. Justice Black bluntly expressed his fear that the Court was claiming for the federal judiciary the "power to invalidate any legislative act which the judges find irrational, unreasonable or offensive."[26]

The issues on which the Court divided in *Griswold* raise vital questions as to the nature of the federal judicial power, and the disagreements are basic. It is therefore important to sift the issues and determine, to the extent possible, whether the constitutional frame on which the new right of privacy was erected invites further expansion into other areas, or whether the platform was a temporary edifice built for this case alone.

Of the many fascinating perspectives from which the several opinions in *Griswold* could be viewed, inquiry will here be limited to three propositions. (1) Does the due process clause of the fourteenth amendment impose any substantive limitations upon state power beyond what can reasonably be found in the "specific" provisions of the Bill of Rights? (2) What is the relationship, if any, between the right of marital privacy and other aspects of the right of privacy, such as the fourth and fifth amendments' prohibitions against unreasonable searches and seizures and against compelled self-incrimination? (3) What, if anything, does *Griswold* foretell of the permissible role of government in the study of population control and, more specifically, in the dissemination of birth control information?

II. FOURTEENTH AMENDMENT DUE PROCESS AND THE BILL OF RIGHTS

There is no specific textual link between any provision of the fourteenth amendment and the protections accorded certain personal liberties in other parts of the Constitution, particularly in the

---

24. *Id.* at 497.
25. *Id.* at 499, 502.
26. *Id.* at 511.

Bill of Rights. It has long been accepted constitutional doctrine, however, that at least "some of the personal rights safeguarded by the first eight Amendments against National action may also be safeguarded against state action, because a denial of them would be a denial of due process of law."[27] Nevertheless, three vital issues centering on the due process clause have caused recurring conflict on the Court.

In the first place, there has been disagreement as to which rights should be deemed applicable to the states through the due process clause. The catalogue of rights thus carried over has expanded rapidly in recent years; by 1965 the Court had ruled applicable to the states all the provisions of the first and fourth amendments, as well as the most significant aspects of the fifth, sixth, and eighth amendments.[28]

A second division of opinion within the Court has involved the question whether those specifics of the Bill of Rights that are regarded as carried over into the due process clause should limit the states to the same extent that they limit the national government. That question has now been resolved in the affirmative,[29] although by no means unanimously.[30]

The third major issue in this area—the issue to which *Griswold* adds new dimension—is the question whether the due process clause not only draws within its prohibitions the fundamental specific provisions of the Bill of Rights but also, by "emanation" or otherwise, limits state governments in additional, largely unspecified ways. This question was raised in 1947 in *Adamson v. California*.[31] In that case the basic issue was whether the due process clause of the fourteenth amendment protects an accused against a state-imposed requirement of testimonial compulsion to the same extent as the fifth amendment privilege against self-incrimination protects an accused against the federal government. A majority of the Court answered in the negative, holding in effect that the privilege against self-incrimination was not carried over into the due process clause of the fourteenth amendment—a holding subsequently overruled

---

27. Twining v. New Jersey, 211 U.S. 78, 99 (1908).
28. The matter is well reviewed in Mr. Justice Brennan's opinion for the Court in Malloy v. Hogan, 378 U.S. 1 (1964). See also Pointer v. Texas, 380 U.S. 400 (1965); Frankfurter, *Memorandum on "Incorporation" of the Bill of Rights Into the Due Process Clause of the Fourteenth Amendment*, 78 HARV. L. REV. 746 (1965); Henkin, *"Selective Incorporation" in the Fourteenth Amendment*, 73 YALE L.J. 74 (1963).
29. See Ker v. California, 374 U.S. 23, 33 (1963).
30. *Id.* at 45 (Harlan, J., concurring).
31. 332 U.S. 46 (1947).

in 1964 in *Malloy v. Hogan*.[32] The dispute as to the possible inclusion of non-Bill of Rights protections within the due process clause of the fourteenth amendment took place among the *Adamson* dissenters. Mr. Justice Black, joined by Mr. Justice Douglas, contended that the due process clause should be read to make the Bill of Rights fully applicable to the states. He rejected not only the doctrine of "selective incorporation," but also the more expansive reading of due process urged by Justices Rutledge and Murphy, also in dissent.[33] While those Justices agreed with the Black-Douglas view "that the specific guarantees of the Bill of Rights should be carried over intact into the first section of the Fourteenth Amendment,"[34] they were "not prepared to say that the latter is entirely and necessarily limited by the Bill of Rights."[35]

The potential for constitutional conflict inherent in the Murphy-Rutledge view of due process became evident in 1952 when, in *Rochin v. California*,[36] all eight members of the Court who participated in the decision agreed that the due process clause forbade the use in evidence of capsules secured from the accused by means of forcible "stomach pumping." There was, however, a significant disagreement over the operative rationale. The majority, through Mr. Justice Frankfurter, thought that this was

> conduct that shocks the conscience. Illegally breaking into the privacy of the petitioner, the struggle to open his mouth and remove what was there, the forcible extraction of his stomach's contents—this course of proceeding by agents of government to obtain evidence is bound to offend even hardened sensibilities. They are methods too close to the rack and the screw to permit of constitutional differentiation.[37]

By this time Justices Murphy and Rutledge were gone, so we cannot know how they would have reacted to this seeming acceptance of their *Adamson* position. But Justices Black and Douglas were quick to point out their fears of unconfined judicial discretion in interpretation of the due process clause. Although Mr. Justice Frankfurter asserted that "the vague contours of the Due Process Clause do not leave judges at large,"[38] Mr. Justice Black urged again his *Adamson* view that a specific constitutional text must be found for

---

32. 378 U.S. 1 (1964). See also Griffin v. California, 380 U.S. 609 (1965).
33. Adamson v. California, 332 U.S. 46, 68 (1947) (Black, J., dissenting).
34. *Id.* at 124.
35. *Ibid.* (Murphy and Rutledge, JJ., dissenting).
36. 342 U.S. 165 (1952).
37. *Id.* at 172.
38. *Id.* at 170.

every constitutional prohibition. For Mr. Justice Black, the fifth
amendment privilege against self-incrimination supplied such a text
in cases where, as in *Rochin*, "incriminating evidence is forcibly
taken from [an accused] by a contrivance of modern science."[39] But,
he said, there is "no express constitutional language granting judicial
power to invalidate *every* state law of *every* kind deemed 'unreasonable' or contrary to the Court's notion of civilized decencies . . . ."[40]
Inevitably, later cases revealed disagreements that could not be
papered over with agreement as to result,[41] and the Black-Douglas
view was strongly reiterated in dissent.

Griswold, however, presented the new phenomenon of the so-
called libertarian result being upheld over the dissent of Mr. Justice
Black, who is often regarded as the leader of the libertarian forces
on the Court. He could find no reasonably express provision in the
Constitution guaranteeing the right of marital privacy, and he could
not agree with Mr. Justice Douglas' suggestion that such a right
could be discovered in the emanations from other provisions. He
rejected the due process argument of Justices Harlan and White
and the ninth amendment rationale of Mr. Justice Goldberg "because on analysis they turn out to be the same thing—merely using
different words to claim for this Court and the federal judiciary
power to invalidate any legislative act which the judges find irrational, unreasonable or offensive."[42]

Although Mr. Justice Black's disagreement with the reasons
given by some of the Justices was not unexpected, surely the matter
calls for further analysis when it is noted that the sole ally for the
Black position was Mr. Justice Stewart, while those most frequently
found in agreement with Black were ranged on the other side in
varying degrees of disagreement.

Mr. Justice Douglas, it will be remembered, had originally
shared Mr. Justice Black's view that due process permits full incorporation of the specifics of the Bill of Rights, but does not permit protections beyond those relatively confined limits. Although Mr. Justice
Douglas emphasized in his opinion for the Court in *Griswold* the
penumbras and emanations from various amendments, he was no-

---

39. *Id.* at 175.
40. *Id.* at 176. Mr. Justice Douglas agreed in a separate concurring opinion, *id.* at
179.
41. See, *e.g.*, Breithaupt v. Abram, 352 U.S. 432 (1957) (blood sample taken from
person rendered unconscious by automobile accident admissible at trial); Irvine v.
California, 347 U.S. 128 (1954) (evidence secured by police through repeated illegal
entries into a home admissible at trial).
42. 381 U.S. at 511.

where specific about the exact *source* of the right of marital privacy. For all of Mr. Justice Black's forgiving reference to a "narrow" disagreement with Mr. Justice Douglas, "relating to the application of the First Amendment to the facts and circumstances of this particular case,"[43] it is difficult to find in the Douglas opinion a basis for even the minimal predictability requisite for constitutional stability. Efforts to define due process in terms of "emanations" seem scarcely more likely to succeed than the somewhat circular efforts to define due process without any external standard more definite than "considerations deeply rooted in reason and in the compelling traditions of the legal profession."[44]

All members of the present Court agree, as presumably all Justices who have sat in the past have agreed, that the Supreme Court has no authority to review the *wisdom* of legislation enacted by Congress or state legislative bodies. To do so would be to infringe upon the legislative domain. Framing the issue in such terms, however, scarcely advances rational resolution of the very real issues that divide the Court. There are three, or perhaps four, views of this matter taken by various members of the Court. Understandably, each group asserts that its way of looking at the matter provides textually supportable answers, whereas other approaches produce rulings based only upon the personal predilections of the judges. The issues thus raised are at the very center of any inquiry into the nature of the judicial process; accordingly, a clear understanding of the implications of the various positions is critically important.

In 1961, in the widely criticized[45] decision in *Poe v. Ullman*,[46] the Supreme Court refused to hear an earlier challenge to the Connecticut anti-contraceptive law, for the stated reason that the case was not ripe for adjudication on the merits. Mr. Justice Harlan made clear in his dissent in *Poe* that he would vote for invalidation of the statute if there should ever be an opportunity to pass on the merits. In discussing the "liberty" protected by the due process clause of the fourteenth amendment, he said:

> This "liberty" is not a series of isolated points pricked out in terms of the taking of property; the freedom of speech, press, and religion; the right to keep and bear arms; the freedom from unreasonable searches and seizures; and so on. It is a rational con-

43. *Ibid.*
44. Rochin v. California, 342 U.S. 165, 171 (1952).
45. See, *e.g.*, 62 COLUM. L. REV. 106 (1962). See also Poe v. Ullman, 367 U.S. 497, 524-39 (1961) (Harlan, J., dissenting).
46. 367 U.S. 497 (1961).

tinuum which, broadly speaking, includes a freedom from all substantial arbitrary impositions and purposeless restraints. . . .[47]

However much other members of the Court objected to the Connecticut law, it seemed likely that the constitutional rationale advanced by Mr. Justice Harlan would not be persuasive to a majority of the Court.[48] Mr. Justice Douglas dissented separately in *Poe*, suggesting a quite different view of due process from that outlined in the Harlan opinion. Perhaps forecasting his later opinion in *Griswold*, Mr. Justice Douglas described "liberty" as "a conception that sometimes gains content from the emanations of other specific guarantees . . . or from experience with the requirements of a free society."[49] Mr. Justice Black dissented from the refusal to reach and decide the merits in *Poe*, but did not join the Douglas dissent. Indeed, in view of Mr. Justice Black's repeated insistence that the due process clause must not be read to limit the states except in ways reasonably inferable from the specifics of the Bill of Rights, it would have been surprising had he joined in the somewhat unguarded talk of emanations in the Douglas opinion.

After 1961 it seemed entirely possible that a review of the Connecticut law on the merits might find a majority of the Court, under the leadership of Mr. Justice Black, unwilling to overturn the statute. With that possibility in mind, opponents of the Connecticut law re-examined the constitutional guarantees to determine whether other arguments could be advanced to persuade the Court to invalidate the Connecticut law. The most plausible rationale was advanced by my colleague Norman Redlich, who reminded the opponents of the statute that the ninth amendment offers shelter to certain rights "retained by the people" and that certain rights are "reserved . . . to the people" by the tenth amendment.[50] Anticipating the charge that these provisions would provide a textual standard no more definite than due process, he argued:

When the question of standards is posed within the context

47. Poe v. Ullman, 367 U.S. 497, 543 (1961) (Harlan, J., dissenting).

48. No one joined in the Harlan dissent in *Poe*, although Mr. Justice Stewart, who agreed with Mr. Justice Harlan on ripeness, said that "in refraining from a discussion of the constitutional issues, I in no way imply that the ultimate result I would reach on the merits of these controversies would differ from the conclusions of my dissenting Brothers [Justices Douglas and Harlan]." *Id.* at 555. Whatever indication of sympathy for the Harlan position there was in that statement vanished when Mr. Justice Stewart dissented in *Griswold*, specifically repudiating the views of both Justices Douglas and Harlan.

49. *Id.* at 517.

50. Redlich, *Are There "Certain Rights . . . Retained by the People"?*, 37 N.Y.U.L. REV. 787 (1962).

of the Ninth and Tenth Amendments, rather than in terms of due process, a definite pattern starts to emerge. To comply with the purposes of these Amendments, the textual standard should be the entire Constitution. The original Constitution and its amendments project through the ages the image of a free and open society. The Ninth and Tenth Amendments recognized— at the very outset of our national experience—that it was impossible to fill in every detail of this image. For that reason certain rights were reserved to the people. The language and history of the two Amendments indicate that the rights reserved were to be of a nature comparable to the rights enumerated. They were "retained . . . by the people" not because they were different from the rights specifically mentioned in the Constitution, but because words were considered inadequate to define all of the rights which man should possess in a free society and because it was believed that the enumeration might imply that other rights did not exist.[51]

On the basis of that reasoning, Professor Redlich was able to argue that the suggested application of these amendments would not resurrect the discredited freedom-of-contract theory of cases like *Lochner v. New York*,[52] which he thought

hardly fits into the scheme of rights set forth in our Constitution. But the right of a married couple to maintain the intimacy of their marital relationship free from the criminal sanction of the state does fit into the pattern of a society which set forth in its national charter that men should be free from unreasonable searches and seizures.[53]

Professor Redlich's suggestion, which invited a detour around sharply divergent views as to the meaning of the due process clause, was adopted by three members of the *Griswold* Court, in Mr. Justice Goldberg's opinion.

[T]he Ninth Amendment shows a belief of the Constitution's authors that fundamental rights exist that are not expressly enumerated in the first eight amendments and an intent that the list of rights included there not be deemed exhaustive. . . . The Ninth Amendment simply shows the intent of the Constitution's authors that other fundamental personal rights should not be denied such protection or disparaged in any other way simply because they are not specifically listed in the first eight constitutional amendments.[54]

51. *Id.* at 810-11.
52. 198 U.S. 45 (1905).
53. Redlich, *supra* note 50, at 811.
54. 381 U.S. at 492. Mr. Justice Douglas also referred to the ninth amendment, but without explanation of its relevance. *Id.* at 484.

There seemed then little more to be done except to establish in some reasonably objective manner that the right to marital privacy was one of the retained "fundamental personal rights." But Mr. Justice Goldberg, in his anxiety to demonstrate that "judges are not left at large to decide cases in light of their personal and private notions,"[55] raised new doubts as to the objectivity of that standard when he cited two cases based on the notion of flexible due process. Quoting from *Snyder v. Massachusetts*,[56] he said that judges "must look to the 'traditions and [collective] conscience of our people' to determine whether a principle is 'so rooted [there] . . . as to be ranked as fundamental.' "[57] He relied on *Powell v. Alabama*[58] for the proposition that "the inquiry is whether a right involved 'is of such a character that it cannot be denied without violating those "fundamental principles of liberty and justice which lie at the base of all our civil and political institutions . . . ." ' "[59]

When Mr. Justice Goldberg thus failed to differentiate between the ninth amendment "retained" rights and the flexible due process concept, it was to be expected that Mr. Justice Black would repudiate the new constitutional canon for the same reasons for which he had always rejected the old. There is indeed much merit in Mr. Justice Black's complaint that the Harlan due process argument and the Goldberg ninth amendment argument "turn out to be the same thing . . . ."[60]

If there is any one proposition on which all members of the Court seem agreed, it is that there must be no return to the philosophy that allowed judicial invalidation on due process grounds of legislation intended to promote economic or social welfare. The Court has repeatedly emphasized that it is not concerned "with the wisdom, need or appropriateness" of legislation.[61] In 1963 Mr. Justice Black wrote a kind of epitaph for that constitutional period in *Ferguson v. Skrupa*: "The doctrine that prevailed in *Lochner, Coppage, Adkins, Burns,* and like cases—that due process authorizes courts to hold laws unconstitutional when they believe the legislature has acted unwisely —has long since been discarded."[62] Justices Black and Stewart saw in *Griswold* a revival of that discarded doctrine. Unfortunately, the

---

55. *Id.* at 493.
56. 291 U.S. 97 (1934).
57. 381 U.S. at 493. ·
58. 287 U.S. 45 (1932).
59. 381 U.S. at 493.
60. *Id.* at 511.
61. Olsen v. Nebraska *ex rel.* Western Reference & Bond Ass'n, 313 U.S. 236, 246 (1941).
62. 372 U.S. 726, 730 (1963).

Douglas and Goldberg opinions are not altogether reassuring that the solutions they proposed are secure against expansion into another period of judicial revisionism.

It is tempting, when the Bill of Rights is not inclusive enough to protect against real or imagined governmental excesses, to search elsewhere for restraints that many believe should be found in a basic charter. Further cases may provide refinement of the ninth amendment view of the retained rights of the people so as to give the requisite certainty and protect against unconfined judicial inventiveness. In this quest for certainty, the tests suggested by Professor Redlich deserve further attention. In areas of general economic and social policy he would have the courts defer to legislative judgment so long as it appears reasonably related to a valid legislative end. But when the legislature extends its action to regulate a right that may be regarded as "an essential ingredient of the free society established by our Constitution,"[63] it is not improper to "require overwhelming proof of necessity and the absence of other and less burdensome means to achieve [the legislative] . . . objectives."[64] He argues that although here—as elsewhere—no purely objective criteria can be established, judges would not be at large; "the Ninth and Tenth Amendments should be used to define rights adjacent to, or analogous to, the pattern of rights which we find in the Constitution."[65]

Whether satisfactorily objective standards can be substituted for the purely personal reactions of judges still remains for future demonstration. Depending upon where the philosophy of *Griswold* leads, either the case will gain a respected place in constitutional jurisprudence as the progenitor of a new source of protection for "fundamental personal rights," or it will be cast aside as a judicial experiment that proved unworkable. The answer may depend in part on the future development of the right of privacy itself, the matter with which part III of this article is concerned.

III. THE RIGHT OF PRIVACY AND THE FOURTH AND FIFTH AMENDMENTS

Even before 1965 the right of privacy was a variable concept, describing a variety of interests used by judges "in different senses and for varying purposes."[66] The use of the term implies a value judg-

---

63. Redlich, *supra* note 50, at 812.
64. *Ibid.*
65. *Ibid.*
66. Beaney, *The Constitutional Right to Privacy in the Supreme Court*, [1962] SUP. CT. REV. 212. For a reflective discussion of the contemporary potential of the privacy concept, see Ruebhausen & Brim, *Privacy and Behavioral Research*, 65 COLUM. L. REV. 1184 (1965).

ment that any invasion of that "right" is somehow wrong and should be resisted. The difficulty is that the notion of a right of privacy has been invoked as often as the proverbial cry of "wolf." Its meaning, if it was ever clear, has become diluted and uncertain through over-generous application to a wide variety of situations. To determine the likely generative impact of the right of privacy as applied in *Griswold*, it is necessary to know more of the origins, development, and current significance of the term.

A. *The Right of Privacy in Constitutional History*

In the United States the principal development of the constitutionally protected right of privacy has been in connection with limitations imposed on the authority of government to seize persons or property. It is familiar history that before the American Revolution the practice had been prevalent in the colonies of issuing to revenue officers "writs of assistance" that empowered them in their discretion to search suspicious places for smuggled goods.[67] In 1761 James Otis denounced the writs because they placed "the liberty of every man in the hands of every petty officer."[68] Of the debate in which that remark was made, John Adams was later to declare that "then and there the child Independence was born."[69]

By 1765 the famous ruling in *Entick v. Carrington*[70] had fixed the course of English law against the search of homes for incriminating evidence pursuant to a general writ or other discretionary exercise of official authority. Thus was constitutional protection given to a right of privacy against seizure of person or property, but ordinarily in terms of property concepts, such as protection against trespass.

This great right, translated into the fourth amendment to the Constitution of the United States as a protection against unreasonable searches and seizures, has been zealously defended; but when this privacy right has been successfully invoked, it has usually been in the context of protection against the unreasonable search and seizure of persons or tangible property. Even in *Boyd v. United States*,[71] when the fourth amendment and the fifth amendment's privilege against self-incrimination were said to "run almost into each

---

67. The relevant history is recapitulated in Boyd v. United States, 116 U.S. 616, 624-31 (1886). See also LASSON, HISTORY AND DEVELOPMENT OF THE FOURTH AMENDMENT TO THE UNITED STATES CONSTITUTION (1937); Barrett, *Personal Rights, Property Rights, and the Fourth Amendment*, [1960] SUP. CT. REV. 46.

68. Quoted in Boyd v. United States, *supra* note 67, at 625.

69. *Ibid.*

70. 19 Howell's State Trials 1029.

71. 116 U.S. 616 (1886).

other,"[72] the factual situation involved a statutory authorization to compel the production of private papers or to have their presumed contents taken as confessed against the person withholding them. Similarly, when the exclusionary rule under the fourth amendment was applied to the states in *Mapp v. Ohio*,[73] the problem again involved a seizure of tangible property.

These cases are linked to *Griswold* only by use of the term "right of privacy" to apply to both types of rights. If, then, the right of marital privacy is to be regarded as an emanation from the Bill of Rights, or if it is a right retained by the people pursuant to the ninth amendment, the question that naturally arises is whether there are other "rights of privacy," hitherto unprotected—perhaps not yet even discovered—that might now come within this more commodious constitutional shelter.

Candidates for constitutional protection as part of the right of privacy are not wanting. The privacy claim had earlier been unsuccessfully invoked in a number of cases. Those situations should now be re-examined to see if they meet the new standard. Perhaps, too, this inquiry may throw some light on the question whether the newly discovered right of marital privacy has a generative potential for other, heretofore untested, situations.

B. *Privacy, Wiretapping, and Eavesdropping*

The most celebrated instance in which the Supreme Court has applied the protection-of-property rationale of the fourth amendment to deny expansion of the amendment's protection into other areas of privacy is *Olmstead v. United States*.[74] In holding that the fourth amendment does not prohibit the use of evidence secured by wiretapping, Mr. Chief Justice Taft emphasized the "property" aspects of the amendment's protective reach:

> The Amendment itself shows that the search is to be of material things—the person, the house, his papers or his effects. The description of the warrant necessary to make the proceeding lawful, is that it must specify the place to be searched and the person or *things* to be seized. . . . The language of the Amendment can not be extended and expanded to include telephone wires reaching to the whole world from the defendant's house or office.[75]

---

72. *Id.* at 630.
73. 367 U.S. 643 (1961). *Cf.* Wong Sun v. United States, 371 U.S. 471 (1963); Silverman v. United States, 365 U.S. 505 (1961).
74. 277 U.S. 438 (1928).
75. *Id.* at 464-65.

The dissents of Justices Brandeis and Holmes, although neither then nor since persuasive to a majority of the Court on this specific issue, have much in common with the Douglas and Goldberg opinions in *Griswold*. In his brief dissent, Mr. Justice Holmes acknowledged the possibility "that the penumbra of the Fourth and Fifth Amendments"[76] should be applied to forbid the wiretapping and the use in evidence of its fruits. But it was the eloquent, oft-quoted dissent of Mr. Justice Brandeis that came closest to the views announced in *Griswold* in 1965. Arguing for an interpretation of the Constitution that would keep its prohibitions abreast of current developments, he pointed out that "subtler and more far-reaching means of invading privacy have become available to the Government. Discovery and invention have made it possible for the Government, by means far more effective than stretching upon the rack, to obtain disclosure in court of what is whispered in the closet."[77]

Brandeis saw the fourth amendment as a basic charter of freedom from governmental intrusion into private affairs. In the most famous passage of his dissent he said:

> The makers of our Constitution undertook to secure conditions favorable to the pursuit of happiness. . . . They conferred, as against the Government, the right to be let alone—the most comprehensive of rights and the right most valued by civilized men. To protect that right, every unjustifiable intrusion by the Government upon the privacy of the individual, whatever the means employed, must be deemed a violation of the Fourth Amendment. And the use, as evidence in a criminal proceeding, of facts ascertained by such intrusion must be deemed a violation of the Fifth.[78]

Closely related to the wiretapping question involved in *Olmstead* is the right of privacy claim raised—and rejected—in the eavesdropping cases. In electronic eavesdropping, which has been described as "the ultimate invasion of privacy,"[79] the fears of Brandeis have come alive. Any telephone can be quickly transformed

---

76. *Id.* at 469.
77. *Id.* at 473. See Brandeis & Warren, *The Right to Privacy*, 4 HARV. L. REV. 193, 195 (1890): "[N]umerous mechanical devices threaten to make good the prediction that 'what is whispered in the closet' shall be proclaimed from the house-tops."
78. Olmstead v. United States, 277 U.S. 438, 478-79 (1928).
79. WILLIAMS, *The Wiretapping-Eavesdropping Problem: A Defense Counsel's View*, 44 MINN. L. REV. 855, 866 (1960). See also DASH, KNOWLTON & SCHWARTZ, THE EAVESDROPPERS 339-79 (1959); PACKARD, THE NAKED SOCIETY (1964); Symposium, *Science and the Law*, 63 MICH. L. REV. 1325 (1965); King, *Electronic Surveillance and Constitutional Rights: Some Developments and Observations*, 33 GEO. WASH. L. REV. 240 (1965); Michael, *Speculations on the Relation of the Computer to Individual Freedom and the Right to Privacy, id.* at 270.

into a microphone which transmits every sound in the room, and so-called parabolic microphones can eavesdrop on a conversation in a room across a hundred-foot-wide street, but there is no constitutional protection against such intrusions.[80] Even the wiretapping prohibitions in section 605 of the Federal Communications Act offer at best limited protection to conversations thought private by their direct participants.[81]

C. *Other Potential Right-of-Privacy Claims*

The privacy argument has been urged and rejected in other cases, but always in relation to some claimed violation of the fourth or fifth amendments—never in connection with Mr. Justice Douglas' "penumbra" concept or Mr. Justice Goldberg's ninth amendment argument. In *Public Utilities Commission v. Pollak*,[82] for example, the Court rejected a claim that radio programs on buses and streetcars of a private company regulated by the District of Columbia invaded the privacy rights of passengers in violation of the due process clause of the fifth amendment. Mr. Justice Douglas was the only dissenter:

> The case comes down to the meaning of "liberty" as used in the Fifth Amendment. Liberty in the constitutional sense must mean more than freedom from unlawful governmental restraint; it must include privacy as well, if it is to be a repository of freedom. The right to be let alone is indeed the beginning of all freedom.
>
> If we remembered this lesson taught by the First Amendment [the "sanctity of thought and belief" as "important aspects of the constitutional right to be let alone"], I do not believe we would construe "liberty" within the meaning of the Fifth Amendment as narrowly as the Court does.[83]

In *Frank v. Maryland*[84] the Court specifically acknowledged that the fourth and fifth amendments protect "the right to be secure from intrusion into personal privacy"[85] and the "intimately related" right of self-protection—"the right to resist unauthorized entry which has as its design the securing of information which may be used to effect a further deprivation of life or liberty or property."[86] But in

---

80. On Lee v. United States, 343 U.S. 747 (1952); Goldman v. United States, 316 U.S. 129 (1942); *cf.* Lopez v. United States, 373 U.S. 427 (1963); Lanza v. New York, 370 U.S. 139 (1962).

81. See generally Westin, *The Wire-Tapping Problem: An Analysis and a Legislative Proposal*, 52 COLUM. L. REV. 165 (1952).

82. 343 U.S. 451 (1952).

83. *Id.* at 467-68. See also DOUGLAS, THE RIGHT OF THE PEOPLE 87 (1958).

84. 359 U.S. 360 (1959).

85. *Id.* at 365.

86. *Ibid.*

that case the action complained against was the demand made by
a municipal health inspector without a search warrant to enter
private premises in search of health hazards. Since no evidence for
criminal prosecutions was sought to be seized, a majority of the
Court denied the existence of any right of privacy sufficient to pre-
clude the search. The four dissenters, in an opinion by Mr. Justice
Douglas, thought that the decision "greatly [diluted] the right of
privacy."[87]

The privacy right has sometimes been discussed by individual
members of the Court, usually in concurring or dissenting opinions,
in connection with rights said to be protected by constitutional provisions other than the fourth and fifth amendments. Thus, it has
been suggested that the first amendment-related freedoms of speech,
conscience, and association are aspects of the right to privacy, because
"the right of privacy implicit in the First Amendment creates an
area into which the Government may not enter."[88] Accordingly,
it has also been suggested that "the interest in privacy as it relates
to freedom of speech and assembly"[89] is sufficiently important to
carry with it a presumption of noninterference by state investigatory
authorities except upon a "showing by the State sufficient to counter-
balance"[90] the privacy right. Similar considerations may also be
relevant for some Justices in other first amendment areas, including
problems arising out of loyalty oaths,[91] admission to the bar,[92]
membership disclosure requirements,[93] and freedom of travel.[94]
But other members of the Court have continued to think of these
matters solely in terms of the first amendment prohibitions, without
considering the potential privacy aspects of the asserted rights. Since
the Court has often been closely divided on these cases, with decisions
wavering from one side to the other of the thin line that divides
governmental power from individual liberties, it is interesting to
speculate whether elevation of the privacy right to majority status
in *Griswold* may also foretell a new way of looking at those aspects

87. *Id.* at 374.
88. Gibson v. Florida Legislative Investigation Comm., 372 U.S. 539, 570 (1963)
(Douglas, J., concurring). See also *id.* at 565, 569.
89. Uphaus v. Wyman, 360 U.S. 72, 107 (1959) (Brennan, J., dissenting).
90. *Ibid.*
91. *E.g.,* Baggett v. Bullitt, 377 U.S. 360 (1964).
92. *E.g.,* Schware v. Board of Bar Examiners, 353 U.S. 232 (1957); Konigsberg v.
State Bar of California, 353 U.S. 252 (1957).
93. *E.g.,* Shelton v. Tucker, 364 U.S. 479 (1960); Bates v. Little Rock, 361 U.S. 516
(1960); NAACP v. Alabama, 357 U.S. 449 (1958).
94. *E.g.,* Aptheker v. Secretary of State, 378 U.S. 500 (1964); Kent v. Dulles, 357
U.S. 116 (1958).

of the right to be let alone that depend on the first amendment for their protection against governmental intrusion.

When the Court has recognized a right of privacy in some context other than the traditional fourth and fifth amendment protection against the taking of property to be used as evidence to aid in criminal prosecutions (and apart from the first amendment areas mentioned above), the privacy concept has sometimes been invoked as a makeweight to help in downgrading claimed invasions of other constitutional rights. Thus, in *Breard v. Alexandria*,[95] the Court upheld an ordinance banning door-to-door solicitation by out-of-state solicitors for magazine subscriptions. The balance was said to be "between some householder's desire for privacy and the publisher's right to distribute publications in the precise way that those soliciting for him think brings the best results."[96] The four dissenters could scarcely see this as a privacy right at all, but as an excuse to downgrade what some saw as first amendment rights[97] and others as the interest in the free flow of interstate commerce.[98]

Another item in this pre-*Griswold* catalogue of privacy rights is *Skinner v. Oklahoma*,[99] in which the Court offered protection against involuntary sterilization pursuant to a statutory authorization that was discriminatory in its application. That judgment, however, rested solely on the equal protection clause of the fourteenth amendment to protect the dignity and personality of the individual.

The short of it is that the right of privacy has been much discussed in the Supreme Court opinions, particularly in recent years, but substantively nothing much came of that discussion until *Griswold*. Except for the fourth amendment holdings, the talk about privacy rights was not supported with judgments in vindication of privacy rights until *Griswold*. Even in the fourth amendment cases, despite an increasing tendency to talk about that amendment's protection of privacy rights the *holdings* seem not to have gone beyond the 1886 decision in *Boyd v. United States*. However closely the fourth and fifth amendments may have been linked by the *Boyd* case, still the constitutional protection did no more than immunize from seizure, real or constructive. The continuing refusal to exclude evidence gained through wiretapping or electronic eavesdropping, and the refusal to apply the fourth amendment to "civil" searches, necessarily demonstrate that the right of privacy, unlike other individual

---

95. 341 U.S. 622 (1951).
96. *Id.* at 644.
97. *Id.* at 649 (Black and Douglas, JJ., dissenting).
98. *Id.* at 645 (Vinson, C.J., and Douglas, J., dissenting).
99. 316 U.S. 535 (1942).

liberty protections, has not significantly adapted itself to developments after 1791.

Griswold does not necessarily foretell evolution in the rather
fixed doctrines of the fourth amendment. The fourth amendment
right of privacy discussed above bears little resemblance to the
right of marital privacy in *Griswold.* For purposes of comparison and
contrast, it may be helpful to think of the fourth amendment right
of privacy as a procedural protection—a limitation upon the means
by which evidence can be obtained for the purpose of securing a
criminal conviction. The right of marital privacy, on the other hand,
is exclusively substantive; when applicable,[100] it nullifies positive law
enacted pursuant to otherwise valid legislative power. Accordingly,
there is no necessary generative force in *Griswold* in relation to the
traditional fourth amendment area.

While it is thus perfectly possible for the two kinds of privacy
to stand entirely apart, never quite touching, it seems more likely
that the new privacy will indeed have an impact on the old. However different from each other they may be, a mutually developing
relationship might be worked out. For example, even if it is conceded that wiretapping and electronic eavesdropping are not violations of the fourth or fifth amendments, the Douglas "penumbra"
argument could be advanced to establish that "emanations" from
the Bill of Rights forbid wiretapping and electronic eavesdropping.
(If this argument seems a bit thin to overcome long-established doctrine—as well it might—the ninth amendment argument may offer
greater promise.) If there is a right to marital privacy in the home,
why should there not be as well a right of privacy in the home or
place of business against the unwelcome intrusion of uninvited participants in conversations intended to be private? If the right of
privacy is not to be limited narrowly to the facts of *Griswold,* but is

---

100. In describing the new right as that of marital privacy, emphasis should apparently be on the word "marital." The concurring opinions by Justices Goldberg and
White state explicitly that the holding "in no way interferes with a State's proper
regulation of sexual promiscuity or misconduct." 381 U.S. at 498-99 (Goldberg, J., concurring); *id.* at 505-07 (White, J., concurring). Mr. Justice Harlan had made the same
point in his dissent in Poe v. Ullman, 367 U.S. 497, 553 (1961), and he adopted those
views in *Griswold,* 381 U.S. at 500 (Harlan, J., concurring). These expressions of will-
ingness to allow the states to continue to forbid adultery, homosexuality, and other
disfavored sexual acts make the result in *Griswold* more acceptable to a society that
has always voiced its public disapproval of sexual nonconformity; they do not, however, make easier the task of the disinterested student of the law who is required to
seek distinctions between the right of marital privacy and the nonright of unwedded
privacy. Perhaps better than anything else this emphasizes that *Griswold* is not a
fourth amendment case. The fourth amendment, after all, protects the privacy of the
home as to illicit activity to the same extent that it protects against disclosure of
innocent activities.

meant to foretell broad protection for the dignity of man and the inviolability of his rights of personality, then should not its applicability be considered in connection with legislative investigations, loyalty oaths, freedom to travel, religious freedom, and other first amendment-related rights?

Far more important than the result on the narrowly special facts of *Griswold* is the question whether the principle there announced can have these important collateral consequences. It is certainly more than a bare possibility.

IV. GOVERNMENT AND THE DISSEMINATION OF BIRTH CONTROL INFORMATION

If the Constitution of the United States is to remain relevant to government in the latter half of the twentieth century, it must provide viable answers to the difficult questions of governmental structure and power. It has already been observed that the *Griswold* case has significance in relation to modern concepts of federalism. Another twentieth century problem is the growing tension between the assumed necessity for a strong state largely devoted to the achievement of social welfare ends and the equally pressing need to preserve the individual from the gathering forces of big government. Intimations from *Griswold* contribute to that continuing dialogue.

Before the Supreme Court decision in *Griswold*, the underlying social issue reflected in that case appeared to be a fairly narrow one. In a 1956 symposium, no one challenged this statement of the then-relevant question: "Should the state prohibit or otherwise regulate the sale or use of contraceptives?"[101] The new question pertinent to the immediate discussion is whether any *government*, state or federal, may disseminate birth control information through public health clinics and social welfare programs in the United States and through international aid programs abroad.

At first impression the problem might not seem very difficult. In states where the giving of birth control information has not raised serious political or religious problems, such information has been made available. Moreover, the once-substantial opposition to the traffic in birth control devices as articles of commerce has been

---

101. *Symposium—Morals, Medicine, and the Law*, 31 N.Y.U.L. REV. 1157, 1158 (1956). Professor Harry Kalven, Jr., almost alone among the contributors to that symposium, noted another question, which he relegated to footnote attention: "A few states now have public birth control clinics. There is perhaps a small issue here as to whether a Catholic taxpayer has any basis for protesting this use of public funds. There is a difference between permitting contraception and sponsoring it." Kalven, *A Special Corner of Civil Liberties—A Legal View*, 31 N.Y.U.L. REV. 1223, 1224-25 n.1 (1956).

gradually eroded.[102] If the states' power to prohibit the use of contraceptives is denied, governmental participation in the information-dispensing process might seem assured. However, a new argument against any governmental role at all in this process has been raised, principally by spokesmen for the Roman Catholic Church.

It is well known that the Catholic Church has long objected on moral grounds to the use of contraceptives. Indeed, in days past Catholic authorities in Massachusetts supported "Vote God's Way" campaigns against repeal of the state's laws prohibiting the dissemination of birth control information. Seeking statutory prohibition even as to non-members of that church was not illogical as a means of attaining religious objectives. So long as anti-use and anti-dissemination statutes could be kept alive, state-supported family planning programs could scarcely be proposed, and even private clinics would operate at the peril of police action.

Gradually, however, Catholic support of these statutes weakened, although without any change in the moral prohibition applicable to members of that church. Indeed, the Catholic Conference on Civil Liberties presented an amicus curiae brief in *Griswold* supporting invalidation, on privacy grounds, of the Connecticut law.

When the Supreme Court based its invalidation of the Connecticut law squarely on the privacy ground, few Catholic leaders expressed public disapproval, and some Catholics identified with the liberal tradition announced cautious approval.[103] Indeed, in a statement that had been approved before release by the National Catholic Welfare Conference, William Ball, general counsel for the Pennsylvania Catholic Conference, had some kind words for the decision.[104] But the focus had by this time shifted. Mr. Ball voiced Conference approval of *Griswold* in the context of his testimony in opposition to a Senate bill[105] which proposed authorization for the United States "more effectively to deal with rapid population growth throughout the world and the problems arising from or connected with such growth. . . ." Catholic critics of the bill feared that it was the first step, not only to promote study of population control, which they

---

102. See Kalven, *supra* note 101, at 1224-29; Ploscowe, *The Place of Law in Medico-Moral Problems: A Legal View*, 31 N.Y.U.L. Rev. 1238, 1240-41 (1956): Comment, *History and Future of the Legal Battle Over Birth Control*, 49 Cornell L.Q. 275 (1964).

103. See Ball, *The Court and Birth Control*, 82 Commonweal 490 (1965). See also N.Y. Times, Aug. 26, 1965, p. 42, col. 1; *id.*, Aug. 29, 1965, p. E5, col. 1.

104. Statement prepared for presentation August 24, 1965, before the Subcommittee on Foreign Aid Expenditures of the Senate Committee on Government Operations (mimeo.).

105. S. 1676 (89th Cong., 1st Sess.).

did not oppose, but also to facilitate governmental efforts to disseminate birth control information at home and abroad.

It is somewhat ironic that the arguments against the bill were based on the new-found friend, the right of privacy. The argument went something like this: For better or for worse, this is the age of the welfare state. The welfare state and its companion, big government, raise problems for the individual, particularly as he seeks to preserve his identity from being submerged into the undifferentiated mass. Grounding of the *Griswold* decision on the right of privacy is said to illustrate again the Supreme Court's concern with individual liberty, already manifested in other areas. It is suggested that the *School Prayer Case*,[106] for example, manifested another facet of the same effort by the Court to protect against governmental intrusion into areas that should remain private. In forbidding state sponsorship of prayers in public schools, the Supreme Court is said to have "found coercion to be inherent in the child-state relationship, even though the project was broadly considered good for children and for society, and even though the child could be exempt by claiming his privilege of non-participation."[107]

We have been reminded of related dangers that lurk in social welfare programs. Professor Charles Reich has pointed out the dangers to privacy in the administration of welfare programs, and he cautions that some welfare regulations attempt "to impose a standard of moral behavior on beneficiaries."[108] Building upon all these concerns, Mr. Ball fears that the use of state power to disseminate birth control information may be regarded as coercive by the recipients. He suggests:

> The reach of the inquisitorial power of the state in the case-worker-client relationship, moreover, raises most serious questions precisely in the area of privacy now constitutionally zoned by the Supreme Court. Does it extend to such matters as frequency of sexual intercourse, ethical outlook, savings habits, drinking habits? What may be made a matter of record, and what guarantees of confidentiality are legally mandated? How far (apart from birth control) may the "planning" in family planning be carried?[109]

Even well-intentioned welfare workers, he fears, may tend to develop

---

106. Engel v. Vitale, 370 U.S. 421 (1962).

107. Statement, *supra* note 104, at 9.

108. Reich, *Individual Rights and Social Welfare—The Emerging Legal Issues,* 74 YALE L.J. 1245, 1247 (1965). See also Reich, *Midnight Welfare Searches and the Social Security Act,* 72 YALE L.J. 1347 (1963).

109. Ball, *supra* note 103, at 493.

a "highly managerial paternalism toward the poor,"[110] based upon "unspoken puritanical assumptions respecting 'undesirables.' "[111]

These suggestions seem alarming at first, but they may be only alarmist. It is doubtless true that there are possibilities for abuse, even serious abuse, in any governmental program. Even as members of disadvantaged groups are especially vulnerable to expressions of governmental hostility, they are also especially likely to misinterpret poorly administered attempts at governmental solicitude. But that is not to say that programs with humanitarian objectives should not be attempted because of the danger of overreaching. The risk involved should instead emphasize the need for careful surveillance of the administration of useful programs that are susceptible to abuse through excess of good will. Difficulties of administration should not be elevated to constitutional status.

Nowhere is the problem more acute than in the area of birth control information. If the dangers are substantial, the needs are equally so. It is perfectly clear that birth control information and anti-contraceptive devices are readily available to the well-to-do and middle classes of American society, where they are widely used. To deny similar information and equal availability to the poor and ill-informed seems likely to add yet another discrimination to those already suffered by the poor. Disadvantage because of poverty is already widespread, and must not be extended. To do so under a claim of privacy would make hollow the victory for individual liberty in *Griswold*.

---

110. *Ibid.*
111. *Ibid.*

PRIVACY IN CONNECTICUT

Arthur E. Sutherland*

OCCASIONALLY a judgment of our Supreme Court, delivered in a superficially petty case, suddenly before our startled eyes displays fundamentals of our constitutional theory. Thus, in *Griswold v. Connecticut*,[1] holding unconstitutional an 1879 Connecticut statute forbidding all persons to use contraceptive devices, the Court found it necessary to discover a "right of privacy" latent in the Bill of Rights and incorporated into the due process clause of the fourteenth amendment. The outcome of the case is satisfying; all nine Justices joined in saying, in one way or another, that Connecticut's statute was nonsense. I am happy to see this limit on public intrusion into private affairs. But the dramatic traits of the case were the necessity felt by five Justices for some comfortingly specific rule in the Constitution which would outlaw Connecticut's statute, and their choice of a "right of privacy" as such a rule. These are five wise and thoughtful judges; one is struck by their sense that they must explain their decision by discovering some pre-existing rule, more definite than "due process" with its vague contours.

From time to time the American intellectual, like all human beings, changes his ideas as to the ideal balance of power in government. Between about 1920 and 1940, wise men at Faculty Club tables and in *New Republic* editorials viewed the federal judiciary with dismay. Throughout this period, the typical academician was a man deeply imbued with faith in majorities. He was certain that all men were inherently good and wise, and that if it were not for the evil machinations of a series of tyrannies, democratic processes would long since have made the world a pleasant place in which to live. There was always some person or organization that was blamed for the non-arrival of Eden: Attorney General Mitchell Palmer, big business, Wall Street, munitions-makers, and, recurrently of course, the Supreme Court of the United States. At that time we felt that if only we could strike off the shackles imposed on majorities by such bad people, mankind, born free but in many places in chains, would again rule itself benignly, and we should all be quite happy.

Between 1938 and 1948, a change of political theory developed in the intellectual life of the United States, a change so profound that men even now hesitate to see it plainly. Some thinkers during

* Bussey Professor of Law, Harvard University.—Ed.
1. 381 U.S. 479 (1965).

that sad decade were revising their evaluation of majoritarian institutions; things done in Germany, Italy, and Russia, as well as certain activity in the United States, had unsettled previous premises of democratic political thinking. Hitler's popularity among the German people, public support of the Un-American Activities Committee and the McCarthy hearings, ancient racial wrongs, recurring state censorship statutes attempting to suppress books which might disturb the social and political ideas of the young—all these brought about a certain amount of revisionism in our ideas about the Supreme Court. Ever since 1905 we academics had poked fun at Mr. Justice Peckham for asking with dismay, "are we all . . . at the mercy of legislative majorities?"[2] In the 1950's these jests of ours came to seem a little less droll than they had a half-century earlier. In 1952 Professor Rostow of the Yale Law School stated our revised credo when he published his distinguished essay, "The Democratic Character of Judicial Review."[3] Upon some of us who had been votaries of unreviewed majoritarianism, there had suddenly burst fearful demonstrations that unrestricted majorities could be as tyrannical as wicked oligarchs. Maybe Peckham's views were not so absurd after all!

This revolution in concepts left us with explanations to make. We still had to sacrifice to the old gods, as men always must. We could not say in so many words that democratic societies should be permitted to produce cruelty, injustice, and stupidity simply because these are traits occasionally exhibited by all mankind. We could not say in plain terms that occasionally we have to select wise and able people and give them the constitutional function of countering the democratic process, at least for a time, until a sober second thought can correct a first thought which had opposite characteristics. To avoid the open challenge to our political faiths involved in appealing from the many to the Nine in order to correct the injustice of the majority, we have sought from time to time to reassure ourselves by repeating the comforting statement that the Supreme Court does not simply say that this or that state or federal measure is so cruel or outrageous that it clashes with an undefinable, but nevertheless effective, constitutional negation of cruelty or outrage. We feel obliged to maintain our abiding democratic orthodoxy by telling ourselves that if we really try hard enough we can rediscover a pre-existing set of hard and fast rules instituted long ago by majority vote of our ancestors, which the Supreme Court has only

2. Lochner v. New York, 198 U.S. 45 (1905).
3. 66 HARV. L. REV. 193 (1952).

to read and apply and which will nullify the outrageous state or federal prescription.

This tension between traditional statements of democratic policy and realism of present-day perceptions emerged in 1947 and 1952 in a classic dialogue between Justices Black and Frankfurter.[4] Mr. Justice Black, seeking to document the existence of certain fundamental rights which must not be violated by the states, found the requisite specifics in the first eight amendments, which he felt were "incorporated" in the fourteenth amendment. Mr. Justice Frankfurter, although dissatisfied with the position of Mr. Justice Black, could find no substitute adequate to explain the revisory function of the Supreme Court. Indeed, Mr. Justice Frankfurter could not bring himself to say, in so many words, that the Court was performing a necessary, albeit anti-democratic, function. In *Rochin v. California*[5] he stoutly affirmed:

> The vague contours of the Due Process Clause do not leave judges at large. We may not draw on our merely personal and private notions and disregard the limits that bind judges in their judicial function. Even though the concept of due process of law is not final and fixed, these limits are derived from considerations that are fused in the whole nature of our judicial process. . . . These are considerations deeply rooted in reason and in the compelling traditions of the legal profession.[6]

The trouble is that Mr. Justice Frankfurter still left us as much at large as we were with mere "due process of law" or with Coke's "common right and reason" in *Doctor Bonham's Case*.[7]

Griswold v. Connecticut is the most recent demonstration of this tension between the necessity for majoritarianism and the aspiration to an undefinable "justice" in government. The extraordinary thing about this case is not its result, but rather the divergencies in the theories of the Justices who wrote the opinions to explain it. Every newspaper reader now knows that the two Connecticut statutes in question provided a fine or imprisonment for the use of any drug or instrument for the purpose of preventing conception, and directed punishment of any person who counseled or assisted another in the use of contraceptive devices, as if he were himself the principal offender. The Connecticut court convicted and fined the

---

4. This debate appeared in Adamson v. California, 332 U.S. 46 (1947), and Rochin v. California, 342 U.S. 165 (1952).

5. 342 U.S. 165 (1952).

6. *Id.* at 169-71. See Cardozo, The Paradoxes of Legal Science (1928); Cardozo, The Growth of the Law (1924); Cardozo, The Nature of the Judicial Process (1921).

7. 8 Co. Rep. 107a, 113b (1610).

Executive Director of the Planned Parenthood League of Connecticut and a cooperating physician for giving information about contraception to married persons. Seven of the nine United States Supreme Court Justices found this state action unconstitutional for a diversity of reasons. The other two, Justices Stewart and Black, expressed the view that this was "an uncommonly silly law . . . obviously unenforceable, except in the oblique context of the present case."[8] Nevertheless, after examining the first, third, fourth, fifth, and ninth amendments, which were relied upon by the various prevailing opinions, the two dissenters found nothing which would invalidate a law proscribing contraceptives. Similarly, they found the due process clause of the fourteenth amendment to be insufficiently explicit to satisfy our aspiration to leave repeal of legislation to legislators.

The opinion of the Court expressed the views of only five Justices —Douglas, Clark, Goldberg, Brennan, and Chief Justice Warren— and the last three felt obliged to add some further views in a separate concurring opinion. Justices Harlan and White did not accept the opinion of the Court, although both agreed that the statute was unconstitutional.

The Court's five-Justice opinion found in the fourteenth amendment certain latent guarantees "penumbral" to the specifics of the Bill of Rights; these penumbral guarantees include "privacy and repose," which were regarded as specific enough to justify the finding of unconstitutionality. The Court's reasoning ran something like this: The fourteenth amendment forbids certain matters which are specified in the first eight amendments. These specifications of the first eight amendments are of two classes—explicit and "penumbral"; in the latter category is a "right of privacy," not mentioned by name in the Constitution, but still an identified and established right. The Court is therefore finding the law, not making it according to its own predispositions, and it is not sitting "as a super-legislature to determine the wisdom, need, and propriety of laws that touch economic problems, business affairs, or social conditions."[9]

To this day, no one knows precisely what the words "due process of law" meant to the draftsmen of the fifth amendment, and no one knows what these words meant to the draftsmen of the fourteenth amendment, or to the many other men who took part in the ratification of either of these provisions. However, the subjective reactions

8. 381 U.S. at 527.
9. *Id.* at 482.

of long-dead constitution-makers are not now significant. What is important is the use which the Supreme Court has made of these words. A common element runs through the several judgments of constitutional invalidity of state action in which states were found to have extorted a confession by long and wearying questions; obtained a confession by fraud; pumped out a man's stomach against his will to provide evidence against him; exposed a school child to schoolroom prayers unwelcome to the child or his parents; censored motion pictures on religious grounds; put a lecturer at a state university in jail until he explained his lectures to the state attorney general; used race as a criterion by which to separate people in public schools even when the education is as good, in objective quality, for one race as it is for another; denied parents the privilege of sending their children to a private rather than a public school; ransacked a doctor's office to find a list of his patients; searched a woman's house and found indecent pictures in a trunk; or punished a physician who gave advice to a husband and wife on how to avoid having unwanted children. The common element is a sense of outrage produced by official pressure on an individual; in the reasoning of the Supreme Court, such pressure produces no good social result and produces undue hardship on the oppressed individual. But is "outraging the Supreme Court's sense of justice" any more definite than "denying due process of law?"

The unspecific quality of this statement of the common element in all these situations raises the question of the Supreme Court's sitting "as a super-legislature to determine the wisdom, need, and propriety of laws." However, it was precisely this characterization of its function which the Court's *Griswold* opinion disclaimed. Not every state measure that arouses a sense of outrage in the minds of some people is unconstitutional; such a rule would render most state legislation invalid. In describing the early nineteenth century concept of the relationship between federal and state power, Mr. Justice Holmes once stated:

> In those days it was not recognized as it is today that most of the distinctions of the law are distinctions of degree. If the States had any power it was assumed that they had all power, and that the necessary alternative was to deny it altogether.[10]

Thus, whereas a great outrage perpetrated by a state violates the due

---

10. Panhandle Oil Co. v. Mississippi *ex rel.* Knox, 277 U.S. 218, 223 (1928) (dissenting opinion). Mr. Justice Holmes was commenting on Mr. Chief Justice Marshall's statement in McCulloch v. Maryland, 17 U.S. (4 Wheat.) 159, 164 (1819), that "the power to tax involves the power to destroy."

process clause of the fourteenth amendment, a small outrage does not, and the Supreme Court of the United States decides when a little becomes too much. Since the difference between too-much and not-too-much is no more definite than the difference between the just and the unjust, pursuit of synonyms for "injustice" is elusive. Shall we then denounce this judicial power? If anyone rebels at the thought of entrusting this power to the nine Justices, he may well consider for a little while to whom he would prefer to entrust it; this can be a sobering experience.

Obviously, some "right of privacy" ought to be guaranteed by the due process clauses. A sensible and rather common modern regulation requires a medical certificate as a precondition to the issuance of a marriage license; but I assume that if some state should require that the necessary medical examination be conducted in public view, no Justice of the Supreme Court would be found to declare this senseless requirement constitutional. The Court might explain this as a violation of "a right of privacy," but just as good an explanation is the outrage perpetrated on the citizen with no compensating benefit.

The Supreme Court has recently been subjected to a great deal of criticism on all sides. Understandably, the Court seeks in its opinions to justify its action by conformity to a tradition of continuity and reliance upon matters already adjudicated. The Supreme Court was clearly right in the *Griswold* result, but there is food for thought in the five Justices' feeling that they had to search for an identifiable, traditional "right of privacy" to justify this decision. Their explanation demonstrates an uneasy sense that a canon of unreasonableness or of injustice is inconsistent with the majoritarian dogma underlying our Constitution and with the tradition that our judges do not make the law, but rather find it all written for them. For this reason, we must continue to pursue the elusive adjective describing that which is constitutionally intolerable. I wish this necessity were not present and that we might, like Justices Harlan and White, rely simply on the idea that such a statute as that in *Griswold* is inconsistent with the undefinable concept of reasonable liberty, which due process of law has come to connote for us and which we must let our nine Justices apply. For this, we must avow when we are frank with ourselves, is our constitutional system.

SUPPLEMENT

Griswold v. *Connecticut*

381 U.S. 479 (1965)

GRISWOLD et al. *v.* CONNECTICUT.

APPEAL FROM THE SUPREME COURT OF ERRORS
OF CONNECTICUT.

No. 496.   Argued March 29–30, 1965.—Decided June 7, 1965.

Appellants, the Executive Director of the Planned Parenthood League
of Connecticut, and its medical director, a licensed physician, were
convicted as accessories for giving married persons information and
medical advice on how to prevent conception and, following examination, prescribing a contraceptive device or material for the wife's
use.   A Connecticut statute makes it a crime for any person to
use any drug or article to prevent conception.   Appellants claimed
that the accessory statute as applied violated the Fourteenth
Amendment.   An intermediate appellate court and the State's
highest court affirmed the judgment.   *Held:*

  1. Appellants have standing to assert the constitutional rights
of the married people.   *Tileston* v. *Ullman*, 318 U. S. 44, distinguished.   P. 481.

  2. The Connecticut statute forbidding use of contraceptives violates the right of marital privacy which is within the penumbra of
specific guarantees of the Bill of Rights.   Pp. 481–486.

151 Conn. 544, 200 A. 2d 479, reversed.

Thomas I. Emerson argued the cause for appellants.
With him on the briefs was *Catherine G. Roraback.*

Joseph B. Clark argued the cause for appellee.   With
him on the brief was *Julius Maretz.*

Briefs of *amici curiae,* urging reversal, were filed by
Whitney North Seymour and *Eleanor M. Fox* for Dr.
John M. Adams et al.; by *Morris L. Ernst, Harriet F.
Pilpel* and *Nancy F. Wechsler* for the Planned Parent-
hood Federation of America, Inc.; by *Alfred L. Scanlon*
for the Catholic Council on Civil Liberties, and by *Rhoda
H. Karpatkin, Melvin L. Wulf* and *Jerome E. Caplan* for
the American Civil Liberties Union et al.

Mr. Justice Douglas delivered the opinion of the Court.

Appellant Griswold is Executive Director of the Planned Parenthood League of Connecticut. Appellant Buxton is a licensed physician and a professor at the Yale Medical School who served as Medical Director for the League at its Center in New Haven—a center open and operating from November 1 to November 10, 1961, when appellants were arrested.

They gave information, instruction, and medical advice to *married persons* as to the means of preventing conception. They examined the wife and prescribed the best contraceptive device or material for her use. Fees were usually charged, although some couples were serviced free.

The statutes whose constitutionality is involved in this appeal are §§ 53–32 and 54–196 of the General Statutes of Connecticut (1958 rev.). The former provides:

> "Any person who uses any drug, medicinal article or instrument for the purpose of preventing conception shall be fined not less than fifty dollars or imprisoned not less than sixty days nor more than one year or be both fined and imprisoned."

Section 54–196 provides:

> "Any person who assists, abets, counsels, causes, hires or commands another to commit any offense may be prosecuted and punished as if he were the principal offender."

The appellants were found guilty as accessories and fined $100 each, against the claim that the accessory statute as so applied violated the Fourteenth Amendment. The Appellate Division of the Circuit Court affirmed. The Supreme Court of Errors affirmed that judgment. 151 Conn. 544, 200 A. 2d 479. We noted probable jurisdiction. 379 U. S. 926.

We think that appellants have standing to raise the constitutional rights of the married people with whom they had a professional relationship. *Tileston* v. *Ullman*, 318 U. S. 44, is different, for there the plaintiff seeking to represent others asked for a declaratory judgment. In that situation we thought that the requirements of standing should be strict, lest the standards of "case or controversy" in Article III of the Constitution become blurred. Here those doubts are removed by reason of a criminal conviction for serving married couples in violation of an aiding-and-abetting statute. Certainly the accessory should have standing to assert that the offense which he is charged with assisting is not, or cannot constitutionally be, a crime.

This case is more akin to *Truax* v. *Raich*, 239 U. S. 33, where an employee was permitted to assert the rights of his employer; to *Pierce* v. *Society of Sisters*, 268 U. S. 510, where the owners of private schools were entitled to assert the rights of potential pupils and their parents; and to *Barrows* v. *Jackson*, 346 U. S. 249, where a white defendant, party to a racially restrictive covenant, who was being sued for damages by the covenantors because she had conveyed her property to Negroes, was allowed to raise the issue that enforcement of the covenant violated the rights of prospective Negro purchasers to equal protection, although no Negro was a party to the suit. And see *Meyer* v. *Nebraska*, 262 U. S. 390; *Adler* v. *Board of Education*, 342 U. S. 485; *NAACP* v. *Alabama*, 357 U. S. 449; *NAACP* v. *Button*, 371 U. S. 415. The rights of husband and wife, pressed here, are likely to be diluted or adversely affected unless those rights are considered in a suit involving those who have this kind of confidential relation to them.

Coming to the merits, we are met with a wide range of questions that implicate the Due Process Clause of the Fourteenth Amendment. Overtones of some arguments

suggest that *Lochner* v. *New York,* 198 U. S. 45, should
be our guide.   But we decline that invitation as we did in
West Coast Hotel Co. v. *Parrish,* 300 U. S. 379; *Olsen* v.
Nebraska, 313 U. S. 236; *Lincoln Union* v. *Northwestern
Co.,* 335 U. S. 525; *Williamson* v. *Lee Optical Co.,* 348
U. S. 483; *Giboney* v. *Empire Storage Co.,* 336 U. S. 490.
We do not sit as a super-legislature to determine the wisdom, need, and propriety of laws that touch economic
problems, business affairs, or social conditions.   This
law, however, operates directly on an intimate relation
of husband and wife and their physician's role in one
aspect of that relation.

The association of people is not mentioned in the Constitution nor in the Bill of Rights.   The right to educate a
child in a school of the parents' choice—whether public or
private or parochial—is also not mentioned.   Nor is the
right to study any particular subject or any foreign
language.   Yet the First Amendment has been construed
to include certain of those rights.

By *Pierce* v. *Society of Sisters, supra,* the right to educate one's children as one chooses is made applicable to
the States by the force of the First and Fourteenth
Amendments.   By *Meyer* v. *Nebraska, supra,* the same
dignity is given the right to study the German language
in a private school.   In other words, the State may not,
consistently with the spirit of the First Amendment, contract the spectrum of available knowledge.   The right of
freedom of speech and press includes not only the right
to utter or to print, but the right to distribute, the right to
receive, the right to read (*Martin* v. *Struthers,* 319 U. S.
141, 143) and freedom of inquiry, freedom of thought,
and freedom to teach (see *Wieman* v. *Updegraff,* 344 U. S.
183, 195)—indeed the freedom of the entire university
community.   *Sweezy* v. *New Hampshire,* 354 U. S. 234,
249–250, 261–263; *Barenblatt* v. *United States,* 360 U. S.
109, 112; *Baggett* v. *Bullitt,* 377 U. S. 360, 369.   Without

those peripheral rights the specific rights would be less secure. And so we reaffirm the principle of the *Pierce* and the *Meyer* cases.

In *NAACP* v. *Alabama,* 357 U. S. 449, 462, we protected the "freedom to associate and privacy in one's associations," noting that freedom of association was a peripheral First Amendment right. Disclosure of membership lists of a constitutionally valid association, we held, was invalid "as entailing the likelihood of a substantial restraint upon the exercise by petitioner's members of their right to freedom of association." *Ibid.* In other words, the First Amendment has a penumbra where privacy is protected from governmental intrusion. In like context, we have protected forms of "association" that are not political in the customary sense but pertain to the social, legal, and economic benefit of the members. *NAACP* v. *Button,* 371 U. S. 415, 430–431. In *Schware* v. *Board of Bar Examiners,* 353 U. S. 232, we held it not permissible to bar a lawyer from practice, because he had once been a member of the Communist Party. The man's "association with that Party" was not shown to be "anything more than a political faith in a political party" (*id.,* at 244) and was not action of a kind proving bad moral character. *Id.,* at 245–246.

Those cases involved more than the "right of assembly"—a right that extends to all irrespective of their race or ideology. *De Jonge* v. *Oregon,* 299 U. S. 353. The right of "association," like the right of belief (*Board of Education* v. *Barnette,* 319 U. S. 624), is more than the right to attend a meeting; it includes the right to express one's attitudes or philosophies by membership in a group or by affiliation with it or by other lawful means. Association in that context is a form of expression of opinion; and while it is not expressly included in the First Amendment its existence is necessary in making the express guarantees fully meaningful.

The foregoing cases suggest that specific guarantees in the Bill of Rights have penumbras, formed by emanations from those guarantees that help give them life and substance. See *Poe* v. *Ullman,* 367 U. S. 497, 516–522 (dissenting opinion). Various guarantees create zones of privacy. The right of association contained in the penumbra of the First Amendment is one, as we have seen. The Third Amendment in its prohibition against the quartering of soldiers "in any house" in time of peace without the consent of the owner is another facet of that privacy. The Fourth Amendment explicitly affirms the "right of the people to be secure in their persons, houses, papers, and effects, against unreasonable searches and seizures." The Fifth Amendment in its Self-Incrimination Clause enables the citizen to create a zone of privacy which government may not force him to surrender to his detriment. The Ninth Amendment provides: "The enumeration in the Constitution, of certain rights, shall not be construed to deny or disparage others retained by the people."

The Fourth and Fifth Amendments were described in *Boyd* v. *United States,* 116 U. S. 616, 630, as protection against all governmental invasions "of the sanctity of a man's home and the privacies of life."* We recently re-

---

*The Court said in full about this right of privacy:

"The principles laid down in this opinion [by Lord Camden in *Entick* v. *Carrington,* 19 How. St. Tr. 1029] affect the very essence of constitutional liberty and security. They reach farther than the concrete form of the case then before the court, with its adventitious circumstances; they apply to all invasions on the part of the government and its employes of the sanctity of a man's home and the privacies of life. It is not the breaking of his doors, and the rummaging of his drawers, that constitutes the essence of the offence; but it is the invasion of his indefeasible right of personal security, personal liberty and private property, where that right has never been forfeited by his conviction of some public offence,—it is the invasion of this sacred right which underlies and constitutes the essence of

ferred in *Mapp* v. *Ohio,* 367 U. S. 643, 656, to the Fourth
Amendment as creating a "right to privacy, no less im-
portant than any other right carefully and particularly
reserved to the people." See Beaney, The Constitutional
Right to Privacy, 1962 Sup. Ct. Rev. 212; Griswold, The
Right to be Let Alone, 55 Nw. U. L. Rev. 216 (1960).

We have had many controversies over these penumbral
rights of "privacy and repose." See, *e. g., Breard* v. *Alexandria,* 341 U. S. 622, 626, 644; *Public Utilities Comm'n*
v. *Pollak,* 343 U. S. 451; *Monroe* v. *Pape,* 365 U. S. 167;
Lanza v. *New York,* 370 U. S. 139; *Frank* v. *Maryland,*
359 U. S. 360; *Skinner* v. *Oklahoma,* 316 U. S. 535, 541.
These cases bear witness that the right of privacy which
presses for recognition here is a legitimate one.

The present case, then, concerns a relationship lying
within the zone of privacy created by several fundamental
constitutional guarantees. And it concerns a law which,
in forbidding the *use* of contraceptives rather than regulating their manufacture or sale, seeks to achieve its goals
by means having a maximum destructive impact upon
that relationship. Such a law cannot stand in light of
the familiar principle, so often applied by this Court, that
a "governmental purpose to control or prevent activities
constitutionally subject to state regulation may not be
achieved by means which sweep unnecessarily broadly
and thereby invade the area of protected freedoms."
NAACP v. *Alabama,* 377 U. S. 288, 307. Would we allow
the police to search the sacred precincts of marital bedrooms for telltale signs of the use of contraceptives? The

---

Lord Camden's judgment. Breaking into a house and opening boxes
and drawers are circumstances of aggravation; but any forcible and
compulsory extortion of a man's own testimony or of his private
papers to be used as evidence to convict him of crime or to forfeit
his goods, is within the condemnation of that judgment. In this
regard the Fourth and Fifth Amendments run almost into each
other." 116 U. S., at 630.

very idea is repulsive to the notions of privacy surrounding the marriage relationship.

We deal with a right of privacy older than the Bill of Rights—older than our political parties, older than our school system.   Marriage is a coming together for better or for worse, hopefully enduring, and intimate to the degree of being sacred.   It is an association that promotes a way of life, not causes; a harmony in living, not political faiths; a bilateral loyalty, not commercial or social projects.   Yet it is an association for as noble a purpose as any involved in our prior decisions.

Reversed.

MR. JUSTICE GOLDBERG, whom THE CHIEF JUSTICE and MR. JUSTICE BRENNAN join, concurring.

I agree with the Court that Connecticut's birth-control law unconstitutionally intrudes upon the right of marital privacy, and I join in its opinion and judgment.   Although I have not accepted the view that "due process" as used in the Fourteenth Amendment incorporates all of the first eight Amendments (see my concurring opinion in *Pointer* v. *Texas,* 380 U. S. 400, 410, and the dissenting opinion of MR. JUSTICE BRENNAN in *Cohen* v. *Hurley,* 366 U. S. 117, 154), I do agree that the concept of liberty protects those personal rights that are fundamental, and is not confined to the specific terms of the Bill of Rights.   My conclusion that the concept of liberty is not so restricted and that it embraces the right of marital privacy though that right is not mentioned explicitly in the Constitution [1] is supported both by numer-

[1] My Brother STEWART dissents on the ground that he "can find no . . . general right of privacy in the Bill of Rights, in any other part of the Constitution, or in any case ever before decided by this Court." *Post,* at 530.   He would require a more explicit guarantee than the one which the Court derives from several constitutional amendments. This Court, however, has never held that the Bill of Rights or the

ous decisions of this Court, referred to in the Court's opinion, and by the language and history of the Ninth Amendment. In reaching the conclusion that the right of marital privacy is protected, as being within the protected penumbra of specific guarantees of the Bill of Rights, the Court refers to the Ninth Amendment, *ante,* at 484. I add these words to emphasize the relevance of that Amendment to the Court's holding.

The Court stated many years ago that the Due Process Clause protects those liberties that are "so rooted in the traditions and conscience of our people as to be ranked as fundamental." *Snyder* v. *Massachusetts,* 291 U. S. 97, 105. In *Gitlow* v. *New York,* 268 U. S. 652, 666, the Court said:

> "For present purposes we may and do assume that freedom of speech and of the press—which are protected by the First Amendment from abridgment by Congress—are among the *fundamental* personal rights and 'liberties' protected by the due process clause of the Fourteenth Amendment from impairment by the States." (Emphasis added.)

Fourteenth Amendment protects only those rights that the Constitution specifically mentions by name. See, *e. g., Bolling* v. *Sharpe,* 347 U. S. 497; *Aptheker* v. *Secretary of State,* 378 U. S. 500; *Kent* v. *Dulles,* 357 U. S. 116; *Carrington* v. *Rash,* 380 U. S. 89, 96; *Schware* v. *Board of Bar Examiners,* 353 U. S. 232; *NAACP* v. *Alabama,* 360 U. S. 240; *Pierce* v. *Society of Sisters,* 268 U. S. 510; *Meyer* v. *Nebraska,* 262 U. S. 390. To the contrary, this Court, for example, in *Bolling* v. *Sharpe, supra,* while recognizing that the Fifth Amendment does not contain the "explicit safeguard" of an equal protection clause, *id.,* at 499, nevertheless derived an equal protection principle from that Amendment's Due Process Clause. And in *Schware* v. *Board of Bar Examiners, supra,* the Court held that the Fourteenth Amendment protects from arbitrary state action the right to pursue an occupation, such as the practice of law.

And, in *Meyer* v. *Nebraska,* 262 U. S. 390, 399, the Court, referring to the Fourteenth Amendment, stated:

> "While this Court has not attempted to define with exactness the liberty thus guaranteed, the term has received much consideration and some of the included things have been definitely stated. Without doubt, it denotes not merely freedom from bodily restraint but also [for example,] the right . . . to marry, establish a home and bring up children . . . ."

This Court, in a series of decisions, has held that the Fourteenth Amendment absorbs and applies to the States those specifics of the first eight amendments which express fundamental personal rights.[2] The language and history of the Ninth Amendment reveal that the Framers of the Constitution believed that there are additional fundamental rights, protected from governmental infringement, which exist alongside those fundamental rights specifically mentioned in the first eight constitutional amendments.

The Ninth Amendment reads, "The enumeration in the Constitution, of certain rights, shall not be construed to deny or disparage others retained by the people." The Amendment is almost entirely the work of James Madison. It was introduced in Congress by him and passed the House and Senate with little or no debate and virtually no change in language. It was proffered to quiet expressed fears that a bill of specifically enumerated rights[3] could not be sufficiently broad to cover all es-

---

[2] See, *e. g., Chicago, B. & Q. R. Co.* v. *Chicago,* 166 U. S. 226; *Gitlow* v. *New York, supra; Cantwell* v. *Connecticut,* 310 U. S. 296; *Wolf* v. *Colorado,* 338 U. S. 25; *Robinson* v. *California,* 370 U. S. 660; *Gideon* v. *Wainwright,* 372 U. S. 335; *Malloy* v. *Hogan,* 378 U. S. 1; *Pointer* v. *Texas, supra; Griffin* v. *California,* 380 U. S. 609.

[3] Madison himself had previously pointed out the dangers of inaccuracy resulting from the fact that "no language is so copious as to supply words and phrases for every complex idea." The Federalist, No. 37 (Cooke ed. 1961), at 236.

sential rights and that the specific mention of certain rights would be interpreted as a denial that others were protected.[4]

In presenting the proposed Amendment, Madison said:

> "It has been objected also against a bill of rights, that, by enumerating particular exceptions to the grant of power, it would disparage those rights which were not placed in that enumeration; and it might follow by implication, that those rights which were not singled out, were intended to be assigned into the hands of the General Government, and were consequently insecure.   This is one of the most plausible arguments I have ever heard urged against the admission of a bill of rights into this system; but, I conceive, that it may be guarded against.   I have attempted it, as gentlemen may see by turning to the

---

[4] Alexander Hamilton was opposed to a bill of rights on the ground that it was unnecessary because the Federal Government was a government of delegated powers and it was not granted the power to intrude upon fundamental personal rights.   The Federalist, No. 84 (Cooke ed. 1961), at 578–579.   He also argued,

"I go further, and affirm that bills of rights, in the sense and in the extent in which they are contended for, are not only unnecessary in the proposed constitution, but would even be dangerous. They would contain various exceptions to powers which are not granted; and on this very account, would afford a colourable pretext to claim more than were granted.   For why declare that things shall not be done which there is no power to do?   Why for instance, should it be said, that the liberty of the press shall not be restrained, when no power is given by which restrictions may be imposed?   I will not contend that such a provision would confer a regulating power; but it is evident that it would furnish, to men disposed to usurp, a plausible pretence for claiming that power."   *Id.*, at 579. The Ninth Amendment and the Tenth Amendment, which provides, "The powers not delegated to the United States by the Constitution, nor prohibited by it to the States, are reserved to the States respectively, or to the people," were apparently also designed in part to meet the above-quoted argument of Hamilton.

last clause of the fourth resolution [the Ninth Amendment]." I Annals of Congress 439 (Gales and Seaton ed. 1834).

Mr. Justice Story wrote of this argument against a bill of rights and the meaning of the Ninth Amendment:

> "In regard to . . . [a] suggestion, that the affirmance of certain rights might disparage others, or might lead to argumentative implications in favor of other powers, it might be sufficient to say that such a course of reasoning could never be sustained upon any solid basis . . . . But a conclusive answer is, that such an attempt may be interdicted (as it has been) by a positive declaration in such a bill of rights that the enumeration of certain rights shall not be construed to deny or disparage others retained by the people." II Story, Commentaries on the Constitution of the United States 626–627 (5th. ed. 1891).

He further stated, referring to the Ninth Amendment:

> "This clause was manifestly introduced to prevent any perverse or ingenious misapplication of the well-known maxim, that an affirmation in particular cases implies a negation in all others; and, *e converso,* that a negation in particular cases implies an affirmation in all others." *Id.,* at 651.

These statements of Madison and Story make clear that the Framers did not intend that the first eight amendments be construed to exhaust the basic and fundamental rights which the Constitution guaranteed to the people.[5]

While this Court has had little occasion to interpret the Ninth Amendment,[6] "[i]t cannot be presumed that any

---

[5] The Tenth Amendment similarly made clear that the States and the people retained all those powers not expressly delegated to the Federal Government.

[6] This Amendment has been referred to as "The Forgotten Ninth Amendment," in a book with that title by Bennett B. Patterson (1955). Other commentary on the Ninth Amendment includes Redlich, Are

clause in the constitution is intended to be without effect." *Marbury* v. *Madison,* 1 Cranch 137, 174. In interpreting the Constitution, "real effect should be given to all the words it uses." *Myers* v. *United States,* 272 U. S. 52, 151. The Ninth Amendment to the Constitution may be regarded by some as a recent discovery and may be forgotten by others, but since 1791 it has been a basic part of the Constitution which we are sworn to uphold. To hold that a right so basic and fundamental and so deep-rooted in our society as the right of privacy in marriage may be infringed because that right is not guaranteed in so many words by the first eight amendments to the Constitution is to ignore the Ninth Amendment and to give it no effect whatsoever. Moreover, a judicial construction that this fundamental right is not protected by the Constitution because it is not mentioned in explicit terms by one of the first eight amendments or elsewhere in the Constitution would violate the Ninth Amendment, which specifically states that

---

There "Certain Rights . . . Retained by the People"? 37 N. Y. U. L. R. v. 787 (1962), and Kelsey, The Ninth Amendment of the Federal Constitution, 11 Ind. L. J. 309 (1936). As far as I am aware, until today this Court has referred to the Ninth Amendment only in *United Public Workers* v. *Mitchell,* 330 U. S. 75, 94–95; *Tennessee Electric Power Co.* v. *TVA,* 306 U. S. 118, 143–144; and *Ashwander* v. *TVA,* 297 U. S. 288, 330–331. See also *Calder* v. *Bull,* 3 Dall. 386, 388; *Loan Assn.* v. *Topeka,* 20 Wall. 655, 662–663.

In *United Public Workers* v. *Mitchell, supra,* at 94–95, the Court stated: "We accept appellants' contention that the nature of political rights reserved to the people by the Ninth and Tenth Amendments [is] involved. The right claimed as inviolate may be stated as the right of a citizen to act as a party official or worker to further his own political views. Thus we have a measure of interference by the Hatch Act and the Rules with what otherwise would be the freedom of the civil servant under the First, Ninth and Tenth Amendments. And, if we look upon due process as a guarantee of freedom in those fields, there is a corresponding impairment of that right under the Fifth Amendment."

"[t]he enumeration in the Constitution, of certain rights, shall not be *construed* to deny or disparage others retained by the people." (Emphasis added.)

A dissenting opinion suggests that my interpretation of the Ninth Amendment somehow "broaden[s] the powers of this Court." *Post*, at 520. With all due respect, I believe that it misses the import of what I am saying. I do not take the position of my Brother BLACK in his dissent in *Adamson* v. *California*, 332 U. S. 46, 68, that the entire Bill of Rights is incorporated in the Fourteenth Amendment, and I do not mean to imply that the Ninth Amendment is applied against the States by the Fourteenth. Nor do I mean to state that the Ninth Amendment constitutes an independent source of rights protected from infringement by either the States or the Federal Government. Rather, the Ninth Amendment shows a belief of the Constitution's authors that fundamental rights exist that are not expressly enumerated in the first eight amendments and an intent that the list of rights included there not be deemed exhaustive. As any student of this Court's opinions knows, this Court has held, often unanimously, that the Fifth and Fourteenth Amendments protect certain fundamental personal liberties from abridgment by the Federal Government or the States. See, *e. g.*, *Bolling* v. *Sharpe*, 347 U. S. 497; *Aptheker* v. *Secretary of State*, 378 U. S. 500; *Kent* v. *Dulles*, 357 U. S. 116; *Cantwell* v. *Connecticut*, 310 U. S. 296; *NAACP* v. *Alabama*, 357 U. S. 449; *Gideon* v. *Wainwright*, 372 U. S. 335; *New York Times Co.* v. *Sullivan*, 376 U. S. 254. The Ninth Amendment simply shows the intent of the Constitution's authors that other fundamental personal rights should not be denied such protection or disparaged in any other way simply because they are not specifically listed in the first eight constitutional amendments. I do not see how this broadens the author-

ity of the Court; rather it serves to support what this
Court has been doing in protecting fundamental rights.

Nor am I turning somersaults with history in arguing
that the Ninth Amendment is relevant in a case dealing
with a *State's* infringement of a fundamental right.
While the Ninth Amendment—and indeed the entire Bill
of Rights—originally concerned restrictions upon *federal*
power, the subsequently enacted Fourteenth Amendment
prohibits the States as well from abridging fundamental
personal liberties. And, the Ninth Amendment, in indi-
cating that not all such liberties are specifically mentioned in the first eight amendments, is surely relevant in
showing the existence of other fundamental personal
rights, now protected from state, as well as federal,
infringement. In sum, the Ninth Amendment simply
lends strong support to the view that the "liberty" protected by the Fifth and Fourteenth Amendments from
infringement by the Federal Government or the States is
not restricted to rights specifically mentioned in the first
eight amendments. Cf. *United Public Workers* v. *Mitchell,* 330 U. S. 75, 94–95.

In determining which rights are fundamental, judges
are not left at large to decide cases in light of their personal and private notions. Rather, they must look to
the "traditions and [collective] conscience of our people"
to determine whether a principle is "so rooted [there] . . .
as to be ranked as fundamental." *Snyder* v. *Massachusetts,* 291 U. S. 97, 105. The inquiry is whether a right
involved "is of such a character that it cannot be denied
without violating those 'fundamental principles of liberty
and justice which lie at the base of all our civil and political institutions' . . . ." *Powell* v. *Alabama,* 287 U. S. 45,
67. "Liberty" also "gains content from the emanations
of . . . specific [constitutional] guarantees" and "from
experience with the requirements of a free society." *Poe*

v. *Ullman,* 367 U. S. 497, 517 (dissenting opinion of MR.
JUSTICE DOUGLAS).[7]

I agree fully with the Court that, applying these tests,
the right of privacy is a fundamental personal right,
emanating "from the totality of the constitutional scheme
under which we live." *Id.,* at 521. Mr. Justice Brandeis,
dissenting in *Olmstead* v. *United States,* 277 U. S. 438,
478, comprehensively summarized the principles underlying the Constitution's guarantees of privacy:

> "The protection guaranteed by the [Fourth and
> Fifth] Amendments is much broader in scope. The
> makers of our Constitution undertook to secure con-
> ditions favorable to the pursuit of happiness. They
> recognized the significance of man's spiritual nature,
> of his feelings and of his intellect. They knew that
> only a part of the pain, pleasure and satisfactions of
> life are to be found in material things. They sought
> to protect Americans in their beliefs, their thoughts,
> their emotions and their sensations. They conferred,
> as against the Government, the right to be let alone—
> the most comprehensive of rights and the right most
> valued by civilized men."

---

[7] In light of the tests enunciated in these cases it cannot be said
that a judge's responsibility to determine whether a right is basic
and fundamental in this sense vests him with unrestricted personal
discretion. In fact, a hesitancy to allow too broad a discretion was
a substantial reason leading me to conclude in *Pointer* v. *Texas, supra,*
at 413–414, that those rights absorbed by the Fourteenth Amendment
and applied to the States because they are fundamental apply with
equal force and to the same extent against both federal and state governments. In *Pointer* I said that the contrary view would require
"this Court to make the extremely subjective and excessively discretionary determination as to whether a practice, forbidden the Federal
Government by a fundamental constitutional guarantee, is, as viewed
in the factual circumstances surrounding each individual case, sufficiently repugnant to the notion of due process as to be forbidden the
States." *Id.,* at 413.

The Connecticut statutes here involved deal with a particularly important and sensitive area of privacy—that of the marital relation and the marital home. This Court recognized in *Meyer* v. *Nebraska, supra,* that the right "to marry, establish a home and bring up children" was an essential part of the liberty guaranteed by the Fourteenth Amendment. 262 U. S., at 399. In *Pierce* v. *Society of Sisters,* 268 U. S. 510, the Court held unconstitutional an Oregon Act which forbade parents from sending their children to private schools because such an act "unreasonably interferes with the liberty of parents and guardians to direct the upbringing and education of children under their control." 268 U. S., at 534–535. As this Court said in *Prince* v. *Massachusetts,* 321 U. S. 158, at 166, the *Meyer* and *Pierce* decisions "have respected the private realm of family life which the state cannot enter."

I agree with MR. JUSTICE HARLAN's statement in his dissenting opinion in *Poe* v. *Ullman,* 367 U. S. 497, 551–552: "Certainly the safeguarding of the home does not follow merely from the sanctity of property rights. The home derives its pre-eminence as the seat of family life. And the integrity of that life is something so fundamental that it has been found to draw to its protection the principles of more than one explicitly granted Constitutional right. . . . Of this whole 'private realm of family life' it is difficult to imagine what is more private or more intimate than a husband and wife's marital relations."

The entire fabric of the Constitution and the purposes that clearly underlie its specific guarantees demonstrate that the rights to marital privacy and to marry and raise a family are of similar order and magnitude as the fundamental rights specifically protected.

Although the Constitution does not speak in so many words of the right of privacy in marriage, I cannot believe that it offers these fundamental rights no protection. The fact that no particular provision of the Constitution explicitly forbids the State from disrupting the traditional relation of the family—a relation as old and as fundamental as our entire civilization—surely does not show that the Government was meant to have the power to do so. Rather, as the Ninth Amendment expressly recognizes, there are fundamental personal rights such as this one, which are protected from abridgment by the Government though not specifically mentioned in the Constitution.

My Brother STEWART, while characterizing the Connecticut birth control law as "an uncommonly silly law," *post*, at 527, would nevertheless let it stand on the ground that it is not for the courts to " 'substitute their social and economic beliefs for the judgment of legislative bodies, who are elected to pass laws.' " *Post*, at 528. Elsewhere, I have stated that "[w]hile I quite agree with Mr. Justice Brandeis that . . . 'a . . . State may . . . serve as a laboratory; and try novel social and economic experiments,' *New State Ice Co.* v. *Liebmann,* 285 U. S. 262, 280, 311 (dissenting opinion), I do not believe that this includes the power to experiment with the fundamental liberties of citizens . . . ." [8] The vice of the dissenters' views is that it would permit such experimentation by the States in the area of the fundamental personal rights of its citizens. I cannot agree that the Constitution grants such power either to the States or to the Federal Government.

The logic of the dissents would sanction federal or state legislation that seems to me even more plainly unconstitutional than the statute before us. Surely the Government, absent a showing of a compelling subordinating state interest, could not decree that all husbands and wives must be sterilized after two children have been born

---

[8] *Pointer* v. *Texas, supra,* at 413. See also the discussion of my Brother DOUGLAS, *Poe* v. *Ullman, supra,* at 517–518 (dissenting opinion).

to them. Yet by their reasoning such an invasion of
marital privacy would not be subject to constitutional
challenge because, while it might be "silly," no provision
of the Constitution specifically prevents the Government
from curtailing the marital right to bear children and raise
a family. While it may shock some of my Brethren that
the Court today holds that the Constitution protects the
right of marital privacy, in my view it is far more shocking
to believe that the personal liberty guaranteed by the
Constitution does not include protection against such
totalitarian limitation of family size, which is at complete
variance with our constitutional concepts. Yet, if upon a
showing of a slender basis of rationality, a law outlawing
voluntary birth control by married persons is valid, then,
by the same reasoning, a law requiring compulsory birth
control also would seem to be valid. In my view, however, both types of law would unjustifiably intrude upon
rights of marital privacy which are constitutionally
protected.

In a long series of cases this Court has held that where
fundamental personal liberties are involved, they may not
be abridged by the States simply on a showing that a
regulatory statute has some rational relationship to the
effectuation of a proper state purpose. "Where there is
a significant encroachment upon personal liberty, the
State may prevail only upon showing a subordinating
interest which is compelling," *Bates* v. *Little Rock,* 361
U. S. 516, 524. The law must be shown "necessary, and
not merely rationally related, to the accomplishment of a
permissible state policy." *McLaughlin* v. *Florida,* 379
U. S. 184, 196. See *Schneider* v. *Irvington,* 308 U. S.
147, 161.

Although the Connecticut birth-control law obviously
encroaches upon a fundamental personal liberty, the State
does not show that the law serves any "subordinating
[state] interest which is compelling" or that it is "neces-

sary . . . to the accomplishment of a permissible state policy." The State, at most, argues that there is some rational relation between this statute and what is admittedly a legitimate subject of state concern—the discouraging of extra-marital relations. It says that preventing the use of birth-control devices by married persons helps prevent the indulgence by some in such extra-marital relations. The rationality of this justification is dubious, particularly in light of the admitted widespread availability to all persons in the State of Connecticut, unmarried as well as married, of birth-control devices for the prevention of disease, as distinguished from the prevention of conception, see *Tileston* v. *Ullman,* 129 Conn. 84, 26 A. 2d 582. But, in any event, it is clear that the state interest in safeguarding marital fidelity can be served by a more discriminately tailored statute, which does not, like the present one, sweep unnecessarily broadly, reaching far beyond the evil sought to be dealt with and intruding upon the privacy of all married couples. See *Aptheker* v. *Secretary of State,* 378 U. S. 500, 514; *NAACP* v. *Alabama,* 377 U. S. 288, 307–308; *McLaughlin* v. *Florida, supra,* at 196. Here, as elsewhere, "[p]recision of regulation must be the touchstone in an area so closely touching our most precious freedoms." *NAACP* v. *Button,* 371 U. S. 415, 438. The State of Connecticut does have statutes, the constitutionality of which is beyond doubt, which prohibit adultery and fornication. See Conn. Gen. Stat. §§ 53–218, 53–219 *et seq.* These statutes demonstrate that means for achieving the same basic purpose of protecting marital fidelity are available to Connecticut without the need to "invade the area of protected freedoms." *NAACP* v. *Alabama, supra,* at 307. See *McLaughlin* v. *Florida, supra,* at 196.

Finally, it should be said of the Court's holding today that it in no way interferes with a State's proper regula-

tion of sexual promiscuity or misconduct.   As my Brother
HARLAN so well stated in his dissenting opinion in *Poe* v.
Ullman, supra, at 553.

> "Adultery, homosexuality and the like are sexual
> intimacies which the State forbids . . . but the
> intimacy of husband and wife is necessarily an essen-
> tial and accepted feature of the institution of mar-
> riage, an institution which the State not only must
> allow, but which always and in every age it has
> fostered and protected.   It is one thing when the
> State exerts its power either to forbid extra-marital
> sexuality . . . or to say who may marry, but it is
> quite another when, having acknowledged a marriage
> and the intimacies inherent in it, it undertakes to
> regulate by means of the criminal law the details of
> that intimacy."

In sum, I believe that the right of privacy in the marital
relation is fundamental and basic—a personal right
"retained by the people" within the meaning of the
Ninth Amendment.   Connecticut cannot constitutionally
abridge this fundamental right, which is protected by the
Fourteenth Amendment from infringement by the States.
I agree with the Court that petitioners' convictions must
therefore be reversed.

MR. JUSTICE HARLAN, concurring in the judgment.

I fully agree with the judgment of reversal, but find
myself unable to join the Court's opinion.   The reason
is that it seems to me to evince an approach to this case
very much like that taken by my Brothers BLACK and
STEWART in dissent, namely: the Due Process Clause of
the Fourteenth Amendment does not touch this Connecticut statute unless the enactment is found to violate some right assured by the letter or penumbra of the
Bill of Rights.

In other words, what I find implicit in the Court's opinion is that the "incorporation" doctrine may be used to *restrict* the reach of Fourteenth Amendment Due Process. For me this is just as unacceptable constitutional doctrine as is the use of the "incorporation" approach to *impose* upon the States all the requirements of the Bill of Rights as found in the provisions of the first eight amendments and in the decisions of this Court interpreting them. See, *e. g.*, my concurring opinions in *Pointer* v. *Texas,* 380 U. S. 400, 408, and *Griffin* v. *California,* 380 U. S. 609, 615, and my dissenting opinion in *Poe* v. *Ullman,* 367 U. S. 497, 522, at pp. 539–545.

In my view, the proper constitutional inquiry in this case is whether this Connecticut statute infringes the Due Process Clause of the Fourteenth Amendment because the enactment violates basic values "implicit in the concept of ordered liberty," *Palko* v. *Connecticut,* 302 U. S. 319, 325. For reasons stated at length in my dissenting opinion in *Poe* v. *Ullman, supra,* I believe that it does. While the relevant inquiry may be aided by resort to one or more of the provisions of the Bill of Rights, it is not dependent on them or any of their radiations. The Due Process Clause of the Fourteenth Amendment stands, in my opinion, on its own bottom.

A further observation seems in order respecting the justification of my Brothers BLACK and STEWART for their "incorporation" approach to this case. Their approach does not rest on historical reasons, which are of course wholly lacking (see Fairman, Does the Fourteenth Amendment Incorporate the Bill of Rights? The Original Understanding, 2 Stan. L. Rev. 5 (1949)), but on the thesis that by limiting the content of the Due Process Clause of the Fourteenth Amendment to the protection of rights which can be found elsewhere in the Constitution, in this instance in the Bill of Rights, judges will thus be confined to "interpretation" of specific constitutional provisions, and will thereby be restrained from introducing their own notions of constitutional right and wrong into the "vague contours of the Due Process Clause." *Rochin* v. *California*, 342 U. S. 165, 170.

While I could not more heartily agree that judicial "self restraint" is an indispensable ingredient of sound constitutional adjudication, I do submit that the formula suggested for achieving it is more hollow than real. "Specific" provisions of the Constitution, no less than "due process," lend themselves as readily to "personal" interpretations by judges whose constitutional outlook is simply to keep the Constitution in supposed "tune with the times" (*post*, p. 522). Need one go further than to recall last Term's reapportionment cases, *Wesberry* v. *Sanders*, 376 U. S. 1, and *Reynolds* v. *Sims*, 377 U. S. 533, where a majority of the Court "interpreted" "by the People" (Art. I, § 2) and "equal protection" (Amdt. 14) to command "one person, one vote," an interpretation that was made in the face of irrefutable and still unanswered history to the contrary? See my dissenting opinions in those cases, 376 U. S., at 20; 377 U. S., at 589.

Judicial self-restraint will not, I suggest, be brought about in the "due process" area by the historically unfounded incorporation formula long advanced by my Brother BLACK, and now in part espoused by my Brother STEWART. It will be achieved in this area, as in other constitutional areas, only by continual insistence upon respect for the teachings of history, solid recognition of the basic values that underlie our society, and wise appreciation of the great roles that the doctrines of federalism and separation of powers have played in establishing and preserving American freedoms. See *Adamson* v. *California*, 332 U. S. 46, 59 (Mr. Justice Frankfurter, concurring). Adherence to these principles will not, of course, obviate all constitutional differences of opinion among judges, nor should it. Their continued recognition will, however, go farther toward keeping most judges from roaming at large in the constitutional field than will the interpolation into the Constitution of an artificial and largely illusory restriction on the content of the Due Process Clause.*

MR. JUSTICE WHITE, concurring in the judgment.

In my view this Connecticut law as applied to married couples deprives them of "liberty" without due process of law, as that concept is used in the Fourteenth Amendment. I therefore concur in the judgment of the Court reversing these convictions under Connecticut's aiding and abetting statute.

It would be unduly repetitious, and belaboring the obvious, to expound on the impact of this statute on the liberty guaranteed by the Fourteenth Amendment against arbitrary or capricious denials or on the nature of this liberty. Suffice it to say that this is not the first time this Court has had occasion to articulate that the liberty entitled to protection under the Fourteenth Amendment includes the right "to marry, establish a home and bring up children," *Meyer* v. *Nebraska,* 262 U. S. 390, 399, and "the liberty . . . to direct the upbringing and education of children," *Pierce* v. *Society of Sisters,* 268 U. S. 510, 534–535, and that these are among "the basic civil rights of man." *Skinner* v. *Oklahoma,* 316 U. S. 535, 541. These decisions affirm that there is a "realm of family life which the state cannot enter" without substantial justification. *Prince* v. *Massachusetts,* 321 U. S. 158, 166. Surely the right invoked in this case, to be free of regulation of the intimacies of

---

*Indeed, my Brother BLACK, in arguing his thesis, is forced to lay aside a host of cases in which the Court has recognized fundamental rights in the Fourteenth Amendment without specific reliance upon the Bill of Rights. *Post,* p. 512, n. 4.

the marriage relationship, "come[s] to this Court with a momentum for respect lacking when appeal is made to liberties which derive merely from shifting economic arrangements." *Kovacs* v. *Cooper,* 336 U. S. 77, 95 (opinion of Frankfurter, J.).

The Connecticut anti-contraceptive statute deals rather substantially with this relationship. For it forbids all married persons the right to use birth-control devices, regardless of whether their use is dictated by considerations of family planning, *Trubek* v. *Ullman,* 147 Conn. 633, 165 A. 2d 158, health, or indeed even of life itself. *Buxton* v. *Ullman,* 147 Conn. 48, 156 A. 2d 508. The anti-use statute, together with the general aiding and abetting statute, prohibits doctors from affording advice to married persons on proper and effective methods of birth control. *Tileston* v. *Ullman,* 129 Conn. 84, 26 A. 2d 582. And the clear effect of these statutes, as enforced, is to deny disadvantaged citizens of Connecticut, those without either adequate knowledge or resources to obtain private counseling, access to medical assistance and up-to-date information in respect to proper methods of birth control. *State* v. *Nelson,* 126 Conn. 412, 11 A. 2d 856; *State* v. *Griswold,* 151 Conn. 544, 200 A. 2d 479. In my view, a statute with these effects bears a substantial burden of justification when attacked under the Fourteenth Amendment. *Yick Wo* v. *Hopkins,* 118 U. S. 356; *Skinner* v. *Oklahoma,* 316 U. S. 535; *Schware* v. *Board of Bar Examiners,* 353 U. S. 232; *McLaughlin* v. *Florida,* 379 U. S. 184, 192.

An examination of the justification offered, however, cannot be avoided by saying that the Connecticut anti-use statute invades a protected area of privacy and association or that it demeans the marriage relationship. The nature of the right invaded is pertinent, to be sure, for statutes regulating sensitive areas of liberty do, under the cases of this Court, require "strict scrutiny," *Skinner* v. *Oklahoma,* 316 U. S. 535, 541, and "must be viewed in the light of less drastic means for achieving the same basic purpose." *Shelton* v. *Tucker,* 364 U. S. 479, 488. "Where there is a significant encroachment upon personal liberty, the State may prevail only upon showing a subordinating interest which is compelling." *Bates* v. *Little Rock,* 361 U. S. 516, 524. See also *McLaughlin* v. *Florida,* 379 U. S. 184. But such statutes, if reasonably necessary for the effectuation of a legitimate and substantial state interest, and not arbitrary or capricious in application, are not invalid under the Due Process Clause. *Zemel* v. *Rusk,* 381 U. S. 1.*

---

*Dissenting opinions assert that the liberty guaranteed by the Due Process Clause is limited to a guarantee against unduly vague statutes and against procedural unfairness at trial. Under this view the Court is without authority to ascertain whether a challenged statute, or its application, has a permissible purpose and whether the manner of regulation bears a rational or justifying relationship to this purpose. A long line of cases makes very clear that this has not been the view of this Court. *Dent* v. *West Virginia,* 129 U. S. 114; *Jacobson* v. *Massachusetts,* 197 U. S. 11; *Douglas* v. *Noble,* 261 U. S. 165; *Meyer* v. *Nebraska,* 262 U. S. 390; *Pierce* v. *Society of Sisters,* 268 U. S. 510; *Schware* v. *Board of Bar Examiners,* 353 U. S. 232; *Aptheker* v. *Secretary of State,* 378 U. S. 500; *Zemel* v. *Rusk,* 381 U. S. 1.

The traditional due process test was well articulated, and applied, in *Schware* v. *Board of Bar Examiners, supra,* a case which placed no reliance on the specific guarantees of the Bill of Rights.

"A State cannot exclude a person from the practice of law or from any other occupation in a manner or for reasons that contravene the Due Process or Equal Protection Clause of the Fourteenth Amendment. *Dent* v. *West Virginia,* 129 U. S. 114. Cf. *Slochower* v. *Board of Education,* 350 U. S. 551; *Wieman* v. *Updegraff,* 344 U. S. 183. And see *Ex parte Secombe,* 19 How. 9, 13. A State can require high standards of qualification, such as good moral character or proficiency in its law, before it admits an applicant to the bar, but any qualification must have a rational connection with the applicant's fitness or capacity to practice law. *Douglas* v. *Noble,* 261 U. S. 165; *Cum-*

As I read the opinions of the Connecticut courts and the argument of Connecticut in this Court, the State claims but one justification for its anti-use statute. Cf. *Allied Stores of Ohio* v. *Bowers,* 358 U. S. 522, 530; *Martin* v. *Walton,* 368 U. S. 25, 28 (DOUGLAS, J., dissenting). There is no serious contention that Connecticut thinks the use of artificial or external methods of contraception immoral or unwise in itself, or that the anti-use statute is founded upon any policy of promoting population expansion. Rather, the statute is said to serve the State's policy against all forms of promiscuous or illicit sexual relationships, be they premarital or extramarital, concededly a permissible and legitimate legislative goal.

Without taking issue with the premise that the fear of conception operates as a deterrent to such relationships in addition to the criminal proscriptions Connecticut has against such conduct, I wholly fail to see how the ban on the use of contraceptives by married couples in any way reinforces the State's ban on illicit sexual relationships. See *Schware* v. *Board of Bar Examiners,* 353 U. S. 232, 239. Connecticut does not bar the importation or possession of contraceptive devices; they are not considered contraband material under state law, *State* v. *Certain Contraceptive Materials,* 126 Conn. 428, 11 A. 2d 863, and their availability in that State is not seriously disputed. The only way Connecticut seeks to limit or control the availability of such devices is through its general aiding and abetting statute whose operation in this context has

_____

mings v. *Missouri,* 4 Wall. 277, 319–320. Cf. *Nebbia* v. *New York,* 291 U. S. 502. Obviously an applicant could not be excluded merely because he was a Republican or a Negro or a member of a particular church. Even in applying permissible standards, officers of a State cannot exclude an applicant when there is no basis for their finding that he fails to meet these standards, or when their action is invidiously discriminatory." 353 U. S., at 238–239. Cf. *Martin* v. *Walton,* 368 U. S. 25, 26 (DOUGLAS, J., dissenting).

been quite obviously ineffective and whose most serious
use has been against birth-control clinics rendering advice
to married, rather than unmarried, persons. Cf. *Yick
Wo* v. *Hopkins*, 118 U. S. 356.   Indeed, after over 80
years of the State's proscription of use, the legality of
the sale of such devices to prevent disease has never been
expressly passed upon, although it appears that sales have
long occurred and have only infrequently been challenged.
This "undeviating policy . . . throughout all the long
years . . . bespeaks more than prosecutorial paralysis."
Poe v. *Ullman*, 367 U. S. 497, 502.   Moreover, it would
appear that the sale of contraceptives to prevent disease
is plainly legal under Connecticut law.

In these circumstances one is rather hard pressed to
explain how the ban on use by married persons in any way
prevents use of such devices by persons engaging in illicit
sexual relations and thereby contributes to the State's
policy against such relationships. Neither the state
courts nor the State before the bar of this Court has
tendered such an explanation.   It is purely fanciful to
believe that the broad proscription on use facilitates discovery of use by persons engaging in a prohibited relationship or for some other reason makes such use more
unlikely and thus can be supported by any sort of administrative consideration.   Perhaps the theory is that the
flat ban on use prevents married people from possessing
contraceptives and without the ready availability of such
devices for use in the marital relationship, there will be
no or less temptation to use them in extramarital ones.
This reasoning rests on the premise that married people
will comply with the ban in regard to their marital relationship, notwithstanding total nonenforcement in this
context and apparent nonenforcibility, but will not
comply with criminal statutes prohibiting extramarital
affairs and the anti-use statute in respect to illicit sexual
relationships, a premise whose validity has not been

demonstrated and whose intrinsic validity is not very evident. At most the broad ban is of marginal utility to the declared objective. A statute limiting its prohibition on use to persons engaging in the prohibited relationship would serve the end posited by Connecticut in the same way, and with the same effectiveness, or ineffectiveness, as the broad anti-use statute under attack in this case. I find nothing in this record justifying the sweeping scope of this statute, with its telling effect on the freedoms of married persons, and therefore conclude that it deprives such persons of liberty without due process of law.

MR. JUSTICE BLACK, with whom MR. JUSTICE STEWART joins, dissenting.

I agree with my Brother STEWART's dissenting opinion. And like him I do not to any extent whatever base my view that this Connecticut law is constitutional on a belief that the law is wise or that its policy is a good one. In order that there may be no room at all to doubt why I vote as I do, I feel constrained to add that the law is every bit as offensive to me as it is to my Brethren of the majority and my Brothers HARLAN, WHITE and GOLD-BERG who, reciting reasons why it is offensive to them, hold it unconstitutional. There is no single one of the graphic and eloquent strictures and criticisms fired at the policy of this Connecticut law either by the Court's opinion or by those of my concurring Brethren to which I cannot subscribe—except their conclusion that the evil qualities they see in the law make it unconstitutional.

Had the doctor defendant here, or even the nondoctor defendant, been convicted for doing nothing more than expressing opinions to persons coming to the clinic that certain contraceptive devices, medicines or practices would do them good and would be desirable, or for telling people how devices could be used, I can think of no reasons at this time why their expressions of views would not be protected by the First and Fourteenth Amendments, which guarantee freedom of speech. Cf. *Brotherhood of Railroad Trainmen* v. *Virginia ex rel. Virginia State Bar,* 377 U. S. 1; *NAACP* v. *Button,* 371 U. S. 415. But speech is one thing; conduct and physical activities are quite another. See, *e. g., Cox* v. *Louisiana,* 379 U. S. 536, 554–555; *Cox* v. *Louisiana,* 379 U. S. 559, 563–564; *id.,* 575–584 (concurring opinion); *Giboney* v. *Empire Storage & Ice Co.,* 336 U. S. 490; cf. *Reynolds* v. *United States,* 98 U. S. 145, 163–164. The two defendants here were active participants in an organization which gave physical examinations to women, advised them what kind of contraceptive devices or medicines would most likely be satisfactory for them, and then supplied the devices themselves, all for a graduated scale of fees, based on the family income. Thus these defendants admittedly engaged with others in a planned course of conduct to help people violate the Connecticut law. Merely because some speech was used in carrying on that conduct—just as in ordinary life some speech accompanies most kinds of conduct—we are not in my view justified in holding that the First Amendment forbids the State to punish their conduct. Strongly as I desire to protect all First Amendment freedoms, I am unable to stretch the Amendment so as to afford protection to the conduct of these defendants in violating the Connecticut law. What would be the constitutional fate of the law if hereafter applied to punish nothing but speech is, as I have said, quite another matter.

The Court talks about a constitutional "right of privacy" as though there is some constitutional provision or provisions forbidding any law ever to be passed which might abridge the "privacy" of individuals. But there is not. There are, of course, guarantees in certain specific constitutional provisions which are designed in part to protect privacy at certain times and places with respect to certain activities. Such, for example, is the Fourth

Amendment's guarantee against "unreasonable searches
and seizures."   But I think it belittles that Amendment
to talk about it as though it protects nothing but "privacy."   To treat it that way is to give it a niggardly interpretation, not the kind of liberal reading I think any Bill
of Rights provision should be given.   The average man
would very likely not have his feelings soothed any more
by having his property seized openly than by having it
seized privately and by stealth.   He simply wants his
property left alone.   And a person can be just as much,
if not more, irritated, annoyed and injured by an unceremonious public arrest by a policeman as he is by a seizure
in the privacy of his office or home.

One of the most effective ways of diluting or expanding
a constitutionally guaranteed right is to substitute for
the crucial word or words of a constitutional guarantee
another word or words, more or less flexible and more or
less restricted in meaning.   This fact is well illustrated by
the use of the term "right of privacy" as a comprehensive
substitute for the Fourth Amendment's guarantee against
"unreasonable searches and seizures."   "Privacy" is a
broad, abstract and ambiguous concept which can easily
be shrunken in meaning but which can also, on the other
hand, easily be interpreted as a constitutional ban against
many things other than searches and seizures.   I have expressed the view many times that First Amendment freedoms, for example, have suffered from a failure of the
courts to stick to the simple language of the First Amendment in construing it, instead of invoking multitudes of
words substituted for those the Framers used.   See, _e. g.,_
New York Times Co. v. _Sullivan,_ 376 U. S. 254, 293 (concurring opinion); cases collected in _City of El Paso_ v.
Simmons, 379 U. S. 497, 517, n. 1 (dissenting opinion);
Black, The Bill of Rights, 35 N. Y. U. L. Rev. 865.   For
these reasons I get nowhere in this case by talk about a
constitutional "right of privacy" as an emanation from

one or more constitutional provisions.[1]   I like my privacy
as well as the next one, but I am nevertheless compelled
to admit that government has a right to invade it unless
prohibited by some specific constitutional provision.   For
these reasons I cannot agree with the Court's judgment
and the reasons it gives for holding this Connecticut law
unconstitutional.

This brings me to the arguments made by my Brothers
HARLAN, WHITE and GOLDBERG for invalidating the Connecticut law.   Brothers HARLAN [2] and WHITE would invalidate it by reliance on the Due Process Clause of the
Fourteenth Amendment, but Brother GOLDBERG, while
agreeing with Brother HARLAN, relies also on the Ninth
Amendment.   I have no doubt that the Connecticut law
could be applied in such a way as to abridge freedom of

---

[1] The phrase "right to privacy" appears first to have gained cur-
rency from an article written by Messrs. Warren and (later Mr. Justice) Brandeis in 1890 which urged that States should give some form
of tort relief to persons whose private affairs were exploited by others.
The Right to Privacy, 4 Harv. L. Rev. 193.   Largely as a result of
this article, some States have passed statutes creating such a cause
of action, and in others state courts have done the same thing by
exercising their powers as courts of common law.   See generally 41
Am. Jur. 926–927.   Thus the Supreme Court of Georgia, in granting
a cause of action for damages to a man whose picture had been used
in a newspaper advertisement without his consent, said that "A right
of privacy in matters purely private is . . . derived from natural law"
and that "The conclusion reached by us seems to be . . . thoroughly
in accord with natural justice, with the principles of the law of every
civilized nation, and especially with the elastic principles of the
common law . . . ." Pavesich v. New England Life Ins. Co., 122
Ga. 190, 194, 218, 50 S. E. 68, 70, 80.   Observing that "the right of
privacy . . . presses for recognition here," today this Court, which I
did not understand to have power to sit as a court of common law,
now appears to be exalting a phrase which Warren and Brandeis
used in discussing grounds for tort relief, to the level of a constitutional rule which prevents state legislatures from passing any law
deemed by this Court to interfere with "privacy."

[2] Brother HARLAN's views are spelled out at greater length in his
dissenting opinion in Poe v. Ullman, 367 U. S. 497, 539–555.

speech and press and therefore violate the First and
Fourteenth Amendments. My disagreement with the
Court's opinion holding that there is such a violation here
is a narrow one, relating to the application of the First
Amendment to the facts and circumstances of this
particular case. But my disagreement with Brothers
HARLAN, WHITE and GOLDBERG is more basic. I think
that if properly construed neither the Due Process Clause
nor the Ninth Amendment, nor both together, could
under any circumstances be a proper basis for invalidating the Connecticut law. I discuss the due process
and Ninth Amendment arguments together because on
analysis they turn out to be the same thing—merely using
different words to claim for this Court and the federal
judiciary power to invalidate any legislative act which
the judges find irrational, unreasonable or offensive.

The due process argument which my Brothers HARLAN
and WHITE adopt here is based, as their opinions indicate,
on the premise that this Court is vested with power to
invalidate all state laws that it considers to be arbitrary, capricious, unreasonable, or oppressive, or on this
Court's belief that a particular state law under scrutiny
has no "rational or justifying" purpose, or is offensive to
a "sense of fairness and justice." [3] If these formulas
based on "natural justice," or others which mean the same
thing,[4] are to prevail, they require judges to determine

---

[3] Indeed, Brother WHITE appears to have gone beyond past pro-
nouncements of the natural law due process theory, which at least
said that the Court should exercise this unlimited power to declare
state acts unconstitutional with "restraint." He now says that, instead of being presumed constitutional (see *Munn* v. *Illinois*, 94 U. S.
113, 123; compare *Adkins* v. *Children's Hospital*, 261 U. S. 525, 544),
the statute here "bears a substantial burden of justification when
attacked under the Fourteenth Amendment."

[4] A collection of the catchwords and catch phrases invoked by
judges who would strike down under the Fourteenth Amendment
laws which offend their notions of natural justice would fill many
pages. Thus it has been said that this Court can forbid state action

what is or is not constitutional on the basis of their own
appraisal of what laws are unwise or unnecessary.   The
power to make such decisions is of course that of a legislative body.   Surely it has to be admitted that no provision of the Constitution specifically gives such blanket
power to courts to exercise such a supervisory veto over
the wisdom and value of legislative policies and to hold
unconstitutional those laws which they believe unwise or
dangerous.   I readily admit that no legislative body, state
or national, should pass laws that can justly be given any

which "shocks the conscience," *Rochin* v. *California*, 342 U. S. 165,
172, sufficiently to "shock itself into the protective arms of the Constitution," *Irvine* v. *California*, 347 U. S. 128, 138 (concurring opinion).   It has been urged that States may not run counter to the
"decencies of civilized conduct," *Rochin, supra*, at 173, or "some principle of justice so rooted in the traditions and conscience of our
people as to be ranked as fundamental," *Snyder* v. *Massachusetts*,
291 U. S. 97, 105, or to "those canons of decency and fairness which
express the notions of justice of English-speaking peoples," *Malinski*
v. *New York*, 324 U. S. 401, 417 (concurring opinion), or to "the
community's sense of fair play and decency," *Rochin, supra*, at 173.
It has been said that we must decide whether a state law is "fair,
reasonable and appropriate," or is rather "an unreasonable, unnecessary and arbitrary interference with the right of the individual
to his personal liberty or to enter into . . . contracts," *Lochner* v.
New York, 198 U. S. 45, 56.   States, under this philosophy, cannot
act in conflict with "deeply rooted feelings of the community,"
Haley v. *Ohio*, 332 U. S. 596, 604 (separate opinion), or with "fundamental notions of fairness and justice," *id.*, 607.   See also, *e. g., Wolf*
v. *Colorado*, 338 U. S. 25, 27 ("rights . . . basic to our free society");
Hebert v. *Louisiana*, 272 U. S. 312, 316 ("fundamental principles
of liberty and justice"); *Adkins* v. *Children's Hospital*, 261 U. S.
525, 561 ("arbitrary restraint of . . . liberties"); *Betts* v. *Brady*,
316 U. S. 455, 462 ("denial of fundamental fairness, shocking to
the universal sense of justice"); *Poe* v. *Ullman*, 367 U. S. 497, 539
(dissenting opinion) ("intolerable and unjustifiable").   Perhaps the
clearest, frankest and briefest explanation of how this due process
approach works is the statement in another case handed down today
that this Court is to invoke the Due Process Clause to strike down
state procedures or laws which it can "not tolerate." *Linkletter* v.
Walker, post, p. 618, at 631.

of the invidious labels invoked as constitutional excuses
to strike down state laws. But perhaps it is not too much
to say that no legislative body ever does pass laws without believing that they will accomplish a sane, rational,
wise and justifiable purpose. While I completely subscribe to the holding of *Marbury* v. *Madison,* 1 Cranch
137, and subsequent cases, that our Court has constitutional power to strike down statutes, state or federal, that
violate commands of the Federal Constitution, I do not
believe that we are granted power by the Due Process
Clause or any other constitutional provision or provisions
to measure constitutionality by our belief that legislation
is arbitrary, capricious or unreasonable, or accomplishes
no justifiable purpose, or is offensive to our own notions
of "civilized standards of conduct." [5] Such an appraisal
of the wisdom of legislation is an attribute of the power
to make laws, not of the power to interpret them. The
use by federal courts of such a formula or doctrine or
whatnot to veto federal or state laws simply takes away
from Congress and States the power to make laws based
on their own judgment of fairness and wisdom and trans-
fers that power to this Court for ultimate determination—a power which was specifically denied to federal
courts by the convention that framed the Constitution.[6]

---

[5] See Hand, The Bill of Rights (1958) 70:

"[J]udges are seldom content merely to annul the particular solution before them; they do not, indeed they may not, say that taking
all things into consideration, the legislators' solution is too strong for
the judicial stomach. On the contrary they wrap up their veto in a
protective veil of adjectives such as 'arbitrary,' 'artificial,' 'normal,'
'reasonable,' 'inherent,' 'fundamental,' or 'essential,' whose office usually, though quite innocently, is to disguise what they are doing and
impute to it a derivation far more impressive than their personal
preferences, which are all that in fact lie behind the decision." See
also *Rochin* v. *California,* 342 U. S. 165, 174 (concurring opinion).
But see *Linkletter* v. *Walker, supra,* n. 4, at 631.

[6] This Court held in *Marbury* v. *Madison,* 1 Cranch 137, that this
Court has power to invalidate laws on the ground that they exceed

Of the cases on which my Brothers WHITE and GOLD-
BERG rely so heavily, undoubtedly the reasoning of two of
them supports their result here—as would that of a number of others which they do not bother to name, *e. g.,*

___

the constitutional power of Congress or violate some specific prohibition of the Constitution. See also *Fletcher* v. *Peck*, 6 Cranch 87.
But the Constitutional Convention did on at least two occasions
reject proposals which would have given the federal judiciary a part
in recommending laws or in vetoing as bad or unwise the legislation
passed by the Congress. Edmund Randolph of Virginia proposed
that the President

". . . and a convenient number of the National Judiciary, ought
to compose a council of revision with authority to examine every
act of the National Legislature before it shall operate, & every act
of a particular Legislature before a Negative thereon shall be final;
and that the dissent of the said Council shall amount to a rejection,
unless the Act of the National Legislature be again passed, or that
of a particular Legislature be again negatived by   [original
wording illegible] of the members of each branch." 1 The Records
of the Federal Convention of 1787 (Farrand ed. 1911) 21.

In support of a plan of this kind James Wilson of Pennsylvania
argued that:

". . . It had been said that the Judges, as expositors of the Laws
would have an opportunity of defending their constitutional rights.
There was weight in this observation; but this power of the Judges
did not go far enough. Laws may be unjust, may be unwise, may be
dangerous, may be destructive; and yet not be so unconstitutional as
to justify the Judges in refusing to give them effect. Let them have
a share in the Revisionary power, and they will have an opportunity
of taking notice of these characters of a law, and of counteracting,
by the weight of their opinions the improper views of the Legislature." 2 *id.,* at 73.

Nathaniel Gorham of Massachusetts "did not see the advantage of
employing the Judges in this way. As Judges they are not to be
presumed to possess any peculiar knowledge of the mere policy of
public measures." *Ibid.*

Elbridge Gerry of Massachusetts likewise opposed the proposal for
a council of revision:

". . . He relied for his part on the Representatives of the people as
the guardians of their Rights & interests. It [the proposal] was

Lochner v. *New York,* 198 U. S. 45, *Coppage* v. *Kansas,*
236 U. S. 1, *Jay Burns Baking Co.* v. *Bryan,* 264 U. S.
504, and *Adkins* v. *Children's Hospital,* 261 U. S. 525.
The two they do cite and quote from, *Meyer* v. *Nebraska,*
262 U. S. 390, and *Pierce* v. *Society of Sisters,* 268 U. S.
510, were both decided in opinions by Mr. Justice
McReynolds which elaborated the same natural law due
process philosopy found in *Lochner* v. *New York, supra,*
one of the cases on which he relied in *Meyer,* along with
such other long-discredited decisions as, *e. g., Adams* v.
Tanner, 244 U. S. 590, and *Adkins* v. *Children's Hospital,
supra. Meyer* held unconstitutional, as an "arbitrary"
and unreasonable interference with the right of a teacher
to carry on his occupation and of parents to hire him, a

---

making the Expositors of the Laws, the Legislators which ought never
to be done." *Id.,* at 75.

And at another point:

"Mr. Gerry doubts whether the Judiciary ought to form a part
of it [the proposed council of revision], as they will have a sufficient check agst. encroachments on their own department by their
exposition of the laws, which involved a power of deciding on their
Constitutionality. . . . It was quite foreign from the nature of ye.
office to make them judges of the policy of public measures." 1 *Id.,*
at 97–98.

Madison supported the proposal on the ground that "a Check [on
the legislature] is necessary." *Id.,* at 108. John Dickinson of Dela-
ware opposed it on the ground that "the Judges must interpret the
Laws they ought not to be legislators." *Ibid.* The proposal for a
council of revision was defeated.

The following proposal was also advanced:

"To assist the President in conducting the Public affairs there shall
be a Council of State composed of the following officers—1. The Chief
Justice of the Supreme Court, who shall from time to time recommend
such alterations of and additions to the laws of the U. S. as may in
his opinion be necessary to the due administration of Justice, and
such as may promote useful learning and inculcate sound morality
throughout the Union . . . ." 2 *id.,* at 342. This proposal too was
rejected.

state law forbidding the teaching of modern foreign languages to young children in the schools.[7]   And in *Pierce,*
relying principally on *Meyer,* Mr. Justice McReynolds
said that a state law requiring that all children attend
public schools interfered unconstitutionally with the property rights of private school corporations because it was an
"arbitrary, unreasonable and unlawful interference" which
threatened "destruction of their business and property."
268 U. S., at 536.   Without expressing an opinion as to
whether either of those cases reached a correct result in
light of our later decisions applying the First Amendment
to the States through the Fourteenth,[8] I merely point out
that the reasoning stated in *Meyer* and *Pierce* was the
same natural law due process philosophy which many
later opinions repudiated, and which I cannot accept.
Brothers WHITE and GOLDBERG also cite other cases, such
as *NAACP* v. *Button,* 371 U. S. 415, *Shelton* v. *Tucker,*
364 U. S. 479, and *Schneider* v. *State,* 308 U. S. 147, which
held that States in regulating conduct could not, consistently with the First Amendment as applied to them by
the Fourteenth, pass unnecessarily broad laws which
might indirectly infringe on First Amendment freedoms.[9]
See *Brotherhood of Railroad Trainmen* v. *Virginia ex rel.*

---

[7] In *Meyer,* in the very same sentence quoted in part by my
Brethren in which he asserted that the Due Process Clause gave an
abstract and inviolable right "to marry, establish a home and bring
up children," Mr. Justice McReynolds also asserted the heretofore
discredited doctrine that the Due Process Clause prevented States
from interfering with "the right of the individual to contract." 262
U. S., at 399.

[8] Compare *Poe* v. *Ullman,* 367 U. S., at 543–544 (HARLAN, J.,
dissenting).

[9] The Court has also said that in view of the Fourteenth Amendment's major purpose of eliminating state-enforced racial discrimination, this Court will scrutinize carefully any law embodying a racial
classification to make sure that it does not deny equal protection
of the laws.   See *McLaughlin* v. *Florida,* 379 U. S. 184.

Virginia State Bar, 377 U. S. 1, 7–8.[10] Brothers WHITE
and GOLDBERG now apparently would start from this requirement that laws be narrowly drafted so as not to curtail free speech and assembly, and extend it limitlessly to
require States to justify any law restricting "liberty" as
my Brethren define "liberty." This would mean at the

---

[10] None of the other cases decided in the past 25 years which
Brothers WHITE and GOLDBERG cite can justly be read as holding
that judges have power to use a natural law due process formula
to strike down all state laws which they think are unwise, dangerous,
or irrational. *Prince v. Massachusetts,* 321 U. S. 158, *upheld* a state
law forbidding minors from selling publications on the streets. *Kent* v.
Dulles, 357 U. S. 116, recognized the power of Congress to restrict
travel outside the country so long as it accorded persons the procedural
safeguards of due process and did not violate any other specific constitutional provision. *Schware v. Board of Bar Examiners,* 353 U. S.
232, held simply that a State could not, consistently with due process,
refuse a lawyer a license to practice law on the basis of a finding that
he was morally unfit when there was no evidence in the record, 353
U. S., at 246–247, to support such a finding. Compare *Thompson* v.
City of Louisville, 362 U. S. 199, in which the Court relied in part
on *Schware.* See also *Konigsberg* v. *State Bar,* 353 U. S. 252. And
Bolling v. *Sharpe,* 347 U. S. 497, merely recognized what had been
the understanding from the beginning of the country, an understanding shared by many of the draftsmen of the Fourteenth Amendment,
that the whole Bill of Rights, including the Due Process Clause of
the Fifth Amendment, was a guarantee that all persons would receive
equal treatment under the law. Compare *Chambers* v. *Florida,* 309
U. S. 227, 240–241. With one exception, the other modern cases relied
on by my Brethren were decided either solely under the Equal Protection Clause of the Fourteenth Amendment or under the First Amendment, made applicable to the States by the Fourteenth, some of the
latter group involving the right of association which this Court has
held to be a part of the rights of speech, press and assembly guaranteed by the First Amendment. As for *Aptheker* v. *Secretary of
State,* 378 U. S. 500, I am compelled to say that if that decision was
written or intended to bring about the abrupt and drastic reversal
in the course of constitutional adjudication which is now attributed
to it, the change was certainly made in a very quiet and unprovocative manner, without any attempt to justify it.

very least, I suppose, that every state criminal statute—
since it must inevitably curtail "liberty" to some extent—
would be suspect, and would have to be justified to this
Court.[11]

My Brother GOLDBERG has adopted the recent discovery [12] that the Ninth Amendment as well as the Due
Process Clause can be used by this Court as authority
to strike down all state legislation which this Court thinks

---

[11] Compare *Adkins* v. *Children's Hospital*, 261 U. S. 525, 568
(Holmes, J., dissenting):

"The earlier decisions upon the same words [the Due Process
Clause] in the Fourteenth Amendment began within our memory and
went no farther than an unpretentious assertion of the liberty to follow the ordinary callings. Later that innocuous generality was expanded into the dogma, Liberty of Contract. Contract is not specially
mentioned in the text that we have to construe. It is merely an example of doing what you want to do, embodied in the word liberty.
But pretty much all law consists in forbidding men to do some things
that they want to do, and contract is no more exempt from law than
other acts."

[12] See Patterson, The Forgotten Ninth Amendment (1955). Mr.
Patterson urges that the Ninth Amendment be used to protect unspecified "natural and inalienable rights." P. 4. The Introduction
by Roscoe Pound states that "there is a marked revival of natural
law ideas throughout the world. Interest in the Ninth Amendment
is a symptom of that revival." P. iii.

In Redlich, Are There "Certain Rights . . . Retained by the People"?, 37 N. Y. U. L. Rev. 787, Professor Redlich, in advocating
reliance on the Ninth and Tenth Amendments to invalidate the
Connecticut law before us, frankly states:

"But for one who feels that the marriage relationship should be
beyond the reach of a state law forbidding the use of contraceptives,
the birth control case poses a troublesome and challenging problem
of constitutional interpretation. He may find himself saying, 'The
law is unconstitutional—but why?' There are two possible paths to
travel in finding the answer. One is to revert to a frankly flexible
due process concept even on matters that do not involve specific constitutional prohibitions. The other is to attempt to evolve a new
constitutional framework within which to meet this and similar
problems which are likely to arise." *Id.*, at 798.

violates "fundamental principles of liberty and justice," or
is contrary to the "traditions and [collective] conscience
of our people."   He also states, without proof satisfactory
to me, that in making decisions on this basis judges will
not consider "their personal and private notions."   One
may ask how they can avoid considering them.   Our
Court certainly has no machinery with which to take a
Gallup Poll.[13]   And the scientific miracles of this age
have not yet produced a gadget which the Court can
use to determine what traditions are rooted in the "[col-
lective] conscience of our people."   Moreover, one would
certainly have to look far beyond the language of the
Ninth Amendment [14] to find that the Framers vested in
this Court any such awesome veto powers over law-
making, either by the States or by the Congress.   Nor
does anything in the history of the Amendment offer any
support for such a shocking doctrine.   The whole history
of the adoption of the Constitution and Bill of Rights
points the other way, and the very material quoted by my
Brother GOLDBERG shows that the Ninth Amendment was
intended to protect against the idea that "by enumerat-
ing particular exceptions to the grant of power" to the
Federal Government, "those rights which were not singled
out, were intended to be assigned into the hands of the
General Government [the United States], and were con-

---

[13] Of course one cannot be oblivious to the fact that Mr. Gallup
has already published the results of a poll which he says show that
46% of the people in this country believe schools should teach about
birth control.   Washington Post, May 21, 1965, p. 2, col. 1.   I can
hardly believe, however, that Brother GOLDBERG would view 46% of
the persons polled as so overwhelming a proportion that this Court
may now rely on it to declare that the Connecticut law infringes
"fundamental" rights, and overrule the long-standing view of the
people of Connecticut expressed through their elected representatives.

[14] U. S. Const., Amend. IX, provides:

"The enumeration in the Constitution, of certain rights, shall not
be construed to deny or disparage others retained by the people."

sequently insecure." [15]   That Amendment was passed,
not to broaden the powers of this Court or any other
department of "the General Government," but, as every
student of history knows, to assure the people that the
Constitution in all its provisions was intended to limit the
Federal Government to the powers granted expressly or
by necessary implication.   If any broad, unlimited power
to hold laws unconstitutional because they offend what
this Court conceives to be the "[collective] conscience of
our people" is vested in this Court by the Ninth Amendment, the Fourteenth Amendment, or any other provision
of the Constitution, it was not given by the Framers, but
rather has been bestowed on the Court by the Court.
This fact is perhaps responsible for the peculiar phenomenon that for a period of a century and a half no serious
suggestion was ever made that the Ninth Amendment,
enacted to protect state powers against federal invasion,
could be used as a weapon of federal power to prevent
state legislatures from passing laws they consider appropriate to govern local affairs.   Use of any such broad,
unbounded judicial authority would make of this Court's
members a day-to-day constitutional convention.

I repeat so as not to be misunderstood that this Court
does have power, which it should exercise, to hold laws
unconstitutional where they are forbidden by the Federal
Constitution.   My point is that there is no provision

---

[15] 1 Annals of Congress 439. See also II Story, Commentaries on
the Constitution of the United States (5th ed. 1891): "This clause
was manifestly introduced to prevent any perverse or ingenious mis-
application of the well-known maxim, that an affirmation in particular cases implies a negation in all others; and, *e converso*, that a
negation in particular cases implies an affirmation in all others. The
maxim, rightly understood, is perfectly sound and safe; but it has
often been strangely forced from its natural meaning into the support of the most dangerous political heresies." *Id.*, at 651 (footnote
omitted).

of the Constitution which either expressly or impliedly
vests power in this Court to sit as a supervisory agency
over acts of duly constituted legislative bodies and set
aside their laws because of the Court's belief that the
legislative policies adopted are unreasonable, unwise, arbitrary, capricious or irrational. The adoption of such
a loose, flexible, uncontrolled standard for holding laws
unconstitutional, if ever it is finally achieved, will amount
to a great unconstitutional shift of power to the courts
which I believe and am constrained to say will be bad for
the courts and worse for the country. Subjecting federal
and state laws to such an unrestrained and unrestrainable
judicial control as to the wisdom of legislative enactments
would, I fear, jeopardize the separation of governmental
powers that the Framers set up and at the same time
threaten to take away much of the power of States
to govern themselves which the Constitution plainly
intended them to have.[16]

---

[16] Justice Holmes in one of his last dissents, written in reply to Mr.
Justice McReynolds' opinion for the Court in *Baldwin* v. *Missouri*,
281 U. S. 586, solemnly warned against a due process formula apparently approved by my concurring Brethren today. He said:

"I have not yet adequately expressed the more than anxiety that
I feel at the ever increasing scope given to the Fourteenth Amendment in cutting down what I believe to be the constitutional rights
of the States. As the decisions now stand, I see hardly any limit but
the sky to the invalidating of those rights if they happen to strike
a majority of this Court as for any reason undesirable. I cannot
believe that the Amendment was intended to give us *carte blanche*
to embody our economic or moral beliefs in its prohibitions. Yet
I can think of no narrower reason that seems to me to justify the
present and the earlier decisions to which I have referred. Of course
the words 'due process of law,' if taken in their literal meaning, have
no application to this case; and while it is too late to deny that they
have been given a much more extended and artificial signification,
still we ought to remember the great caution shown by the Consti-

I realize that many good and able men have eloquently spoken and written, sometimes in rhapsodical strains, about the duty of this Court to keep the Constitution in tune with the times. The idea is that the Constitution must be changed from time to time and that this Court is charged with a duty to make those changes. For myself, I must with all deference reject that philosophy. The Constitution makers knew the need for change and provided for it. Amendments suggested by the people's elected representatives can be submitted to the people or their selected agents for ratification. That method of change was good for our Fathers, and being somewhat old-fashioned I must add it is good enough for me. And so, I cannot rely on the Due Process Clause or the Ninth Amendment or any mysterious and uncertain natural law concept as a reason for striking down this state law. The Due Process Clause with an "arbitrary and capricious" or "shocking to the conscience" formula was liberally used by this Court to strike down economic legislation in the early decades of this century, threatening, many people thought, the tranquility and stability of the Nation. See, *e. g.*, *Lochner* v. *New York,* 198 U. S. 45. That formula, based on subjective considerations of "natural justice," is no less dangerous when used to enforce this Court's views about personal rights than those about economic rights. I had thought that we had laid that formula, as a means for striking down state legislation, to rest once and for all in cases like *West Coast Hotel Co.* v. *Parrish,* 300 U. S. 379; *Olsen* v. *Nebraska ex rel. Western Reference & Bond Assn.,* 313 U. S. 236, and many other

tution in limiting the power of the States, and should be slow to construe the clause in the Fourteenth Amendment as committing to the Court, with no guide but the Court's own discretion, the validity of whatever laws the States may pass." 281 U. S., at 595. See 2 Holmes-Pollock Letters (Howe ed. 1941) 267–268.

opinions.[17]   See also *Lochner* v. *New York,* 198 U. S. 45, 74 (Holmes, J., dissenting).

In *Ferguson* v. *Skrupa,* 372 U. S. 726, 730, this Court two years ago said in an opinion joined by all the Justices but one [18] that

> "The doctrine that prevailed in *Lochner, Coppage, Adkins, Burns,* and like cases—that due process authorizes courts to hold laws unconstitutional when they believe the legislature has acted unwisely—has long since been discarded.   We have returned to the original constitutional proposition that courts do not substitute their social and economic beliefs for the judgment of legislative bodies, who are elected to pass laws."

And only six weeks ago, without even bothering to hear argument, this Court overruled *Tyson & Brother* v. *Banton,* 273 U. S. 418, which had held state laws regulating ticket brokers to be a denial of due process of law.[19]   *Gold*

---

[17] *E. g.,* in *Day-Brite Lighting, Inc.* v. *Missouri,* 342 U. S. 421, 423, this Court held that "Our recent decisions make plain that we do not sit as a superlegislature to weigh the wisdom of legislation nor to decide whether the policy which it expresses offends the public welfare." Compare *Gardner* v. *Massachusetts,* 305 U. S. 559, which the Court today apparently overrules, which held that a challenge under the Federal Constitution to a state law forbidding the sale or furnishing of contraceptives did not raise a substantial federal question.

[18] Brother HARLAN, who has consistently stated his belief in the power of courts to strike down laws which they consider arbitrary or unreasonable, see, *e. g., Poe* v. *Ullman,* 367 U. S. 497, 539–555 (dissenting opinion), did not join the Court's opinion in *Ferguson* v. *Skrupa.*

[19] Justice Holmes, dissenting in *Tyson,* said:

"I think the proper course is to recognize that a state legislature can do whatever it sees fit to do unless it is restrained by some express prohibition in the Constitution of the United States or of the State, and that Courts should be careful not to extend such prohibitions beyond their obvious meaning by reading into them conceptions of public policy that the particular Court may happen to entertain." 273 U. S., at 446.

v. *DiCarlo,* 380 U. S. 520.   I find April's holding hard to square with what my concurring Brethren urge today. They would reinstate the *Lochner, Coppage, Adkins, Burns* line of cases, cases from which this Court recoiled after the 1930's, and which had been I thought totally discredited until now.   Apparently my Brethren have less quarrel with state economic regulations than former Justices of their persuasion had.   But any limitation upon their using the natural law due process philosophy to strike down any state law, dealing with any activity whatever, will obviously be only self-imposed.[20]

In 1798, when this Court was asked to hold another Connecticut law unconstitutional, Justice Iredell said:

"[I]t has been the policy of all the *American* states, which have, individually, framed their state constitutions since the revolution, and of the people of the *United States,* when they framed the Federal Constitution, to define with precision the objects of the legislative power, and to restrain its exercise within marked and settled boundaries.   If any act of Congress, or of the Legislature of a state, violates those constitutional provisions, it is unquestionably void; though, I admit, that as the authority to declare it void is of a delicate and awful nature, the Court will never resort to that authority, but in a clear and urgent case.   If, on the other hand, the Legislature of the Union, or the Legislature of any member of the Union, shall pass a law, within the

---

[20] Compare *Nicchia* v. *New York,* 254 U. S. 228, 231, upholding a New York dog-licensing statute on the ground that it did not "deprive dog owners of liberty without due process of law."   And as I said concurring in *Rochin* v. *California,* 342 U. S. 165, 175, "I believe that faithful adherence to the specific guarantees in the Bill of Rights insures a more permanent protection of individual liberty than that which can be afforded by the nebulous standards" urged by my concurring Brethren today.

general scope of their constitutional power, the Court
cannot pronounce it to be void, merely because it is,
in their judgment, contrary to the principles of natural justice.   The ideas of natural justice are regulated by no fixed standard: the ablest and the purest
men have differed upon the subject; and all that the
Court could properly say, in such an event, would be,
that the Legislature (possessed of an equal right of
opinion) had passed an act which, in the opinion of
the judges, was inconsistent with the abstract principles of natural justice." *Calder* v. *Bull,* 3 Dall.
386, 399 (emphasis in original).

I would adhere to that constitutional philosophy in passing on this Connecticut law today.   I am not persuaded
to deviate from the view which I stated in 1947 in
Adamson v. *California,* 332 U. S. 46, 90–92 (dissenting
opinion):

"Since *Marbury* v. *Madison,* 1 Cranch 137, was
decided, the practice has been firmly established, for
better or worse, that courts can strike down legislative enactments which violate the Constitution.
This process, of course, involves interpretation, and
since words can have many meanings, interpretation obviously may result in contraction or extension
of the original purpose of a constitutional provision,
thereby affecting policy.   But to pass upon the constitutionality of statutes by looking to the particular
standards enumerated in the Bill of Rights and other
parts of the Constitution is one thing; to invalidate
statutes because of application of 'natural law'
deemed to be above and undefined by the Constitution is another.   'In the one instance, courts proceeding within clearly marked constitutional boundaries
seek to execute policies written into the Constitution: in the other, they roam at will in the limit-

less area of their own beliefs as to reasonableness and
actually select policies, a responsibility which the
Constitution entrusts to the legislative representatives of the people.' *Federal Power Commission* v.
Pipeline Co., 315 U. S. 575, 599, 601, n. 4." [21]   (Foot-
notes omitted.)

The late Judge Learned Hand, after emphasizing his view
that judges should not use the due process formula suggested in the concurring opinions today or any other
formula like it to invalidate legislation offensive to their
"personal preferences," [22] made the statement, with which
I fully agree, that:

> "For myself it would be most irksome to be
> ruled by a bevy of Platonic Guardians, even if I

---

[21] *Gideon* v. *Wainwright*, 372 U. S. 335, and similar cases applying
specific Bill of Rights provisions to the States do not in my view
stand for the proposition that this Court can rely on its own concept
of "ordered liberty." or "shocking the conscience" or natural law to
decide what laws it will permit state legislatures to enact. *Gideon*
in applying to state prosecutions the Sixth Amendment's guarantee of
right to counsel followed *Palko* v. *Connecticut*, 302 U. S. 319, which
had held that specific provisions of the Bill of Rights, rather than
the Bill of Rights as a whole, would be selectively applied to the
States. While expressing my own belief (not shared by MR. JUSTICE
STEWART) that all the provisions of the Bill of Rights were made
applicable to the States by the Fourteenth Amendment, in my dissent in *Adamson* v. *California*, 332 U. S. 46, 89, I also said:

"If the choice must be between the selective process of the *Palko*
decision applying some of the Bill of Rights to the States, or the
Twining rule applying none of them, I would choose the *Palko* selective process."

Gideon and similar cases merely followed the *Palko* rule, which in
Adamson I agreed to follow if necessary to make Bill of Rights safeguards applicable to the States. See also *Pointer* v. *Texas*, 380 U. S.
400; *Malloy* v. *Hogan*, 378 U. S. 1.

[22] Hand, The Bill of Rights (1958) 70. See note 5, *supra*. See
generally *id.*, at 35–45.

knew how to choose them, which I assuredly do not." [23]

So far as I am concerned, Connecticut's law as applied here is not forbidden by any provision of the Federal Constitution as that Constitution was written, and I would therefore affirm.

MR. JUSTICE STEWART, whom MR. JUSTICE BLACK joins, dissenting.

Since 1879 Connecticut has had on its books a law which forbids the use of contraceptives by anyone. I think this is an uncommonly silly law. As a practical matter, the law is obviously unenforceable, except in the oblique context of the present case. As a philosophical matter, I believe the use of contraceptives in the relationship of marriage should be left to personal and private choice, based upon each individual's moral, ethical, and religious beliefs. As a matter of social policy, I think professional counsel about methods of birth control should be available to all, so that each individual's choice can be meaningfully made. But we are not asked in this case to say whether we think this law is unwise, or even asinine. We are asked to hold that it violates the United States Constitution. And that I cannot do.

In the course of its opinion the Court refers to no less than six Amendments to the Constitution: the First, the Third, the Fourth, the Fifth, the Ninth, and the Four-

---

[23] *Id.,* at 73. While Judge Hand condemned as unjustified the invalidation of state laws under the natural law due process formula, see *id.,* at 35–45, he also expressed the view that this Court in a number of cases had gone too far in holding legislation to be in violation of specific guarantees of the Bill of Rights. Although I agree with his criticism of use of the due process formula, I do not agree with all the views he expressed about construing the specific guarantees of the Bill of Rights.

teenth. But the Court does not say which of these Amendments, if any, it thinks is infringed by this Connecticut law.

We *are* told that the Due Process Clause of the Fourteenth Amendment is not, as such, the "guide" in this case. With that much I agree. There is no claim that this law, duly enacted by the Connecticut Legislature, is unconstitutionally vague. There is no claim that the appellants were denied any of the elements of procedural due process at their trial, so as to make their convictions constitutionally invalid. And, as the Court says, the day has long passed since the Due Process Clause was regarded as a proper instrument for determining "the wisdom, need, and propriety" of state laws. Compare *Lochner* v. *New York,* 198 U. S. 45, with *Ferguson* v. *Skrupa,* 372 U. S. 726. My Brothers HARLAN and WHITE to the contrary, "[w]e have returned to the original constitutional proposition that courts do not substitute their social and economic beliefs for the judgment of legislative bodies, who are elected to pass laws." *Ferguson* v. *Skrupa, supra,* at 730.

As to the First, Third, Fourth, and Fifth Amendments, I can find nothing in any of them to invalidate this Connecticut law, even assuming that all those Amendments are fully applicable against the States.[1] It has

---

[1] The Amendments in question were, as everyone knows, originally adopted as limitations upon the power of the newly created Federal Government, not as limitations upon the powers of the individual States. But the Court has held that many of the provisions of the first eight amendments are fully embraced by the Fourteenth Amendment as limitations upon state action, and some members of the Court have held the view that the adoption of the Fourteenth Amendment made every provision of the first eight amendments fully applicable against the States. See *Adamson* v. *California,* 332 U. S. 46, 68 (dissenting opinion of MR. JUSTICE BLACK).

not even been argued that this is a law "respecting an establishment of religion, or prohibiting the free exercise thereof." [2]   And surely, unless the solemn process of constitutional adjudication is to descend to the level of a play on words, there is not involved here any abridgment of "the freedom of speech, or of the press; or the right of the people peaceably to assemble, and to petition the Government for a redress of grievances." [3]   No soldier has been quartered in any house.[4]   There has been no search, and no seizure.[5]   Nobody has been compelled to be a witness against himself.[6]

The Court also quotes the Ninth Amendment, and my Brother GOLDBERG's concurring opinion relies heavily upon it.   But to say that the Ninth Amendment has anything to do with this case is to turn somersaults with history. The Ninth Amendment, like its companion the Tenth, which this Court held "states but a truism that all is retained which has not been surrendered," *United States* v. *Darby,* 312 U. S. 100, 124, was framed by James Madison and adopted by the States simply to make clear that the adoption of the Bill of Rights did not alter the plan that

---

[2] U. S. Constitution, Amendment I.   To be sure, the injunction contained in the Connecticut statute coincides with the doctrine of certain religious faiths.   But if that were enough to invalidate a law under the provisions of the First Amendment relating to religion, then most criminal laws would be invalidated.   See, *e. g.,* the Ten Commandments.   The Bible, Exodus 20:2–17 (King James).

[3] U. S. Constitution, Amendment I.   If all the appellants had done was to advise people that they thought the use of contraceptives was desirable, or even to counsel their use, the appellants would, of course, have a substantial First Amendment claim.   But their activities went far beyond mere advocacy.   They prescribed specific contraceptive devices and furnished patients with the prescribed contraceptive materials.

[4] U. S. Constitution, Amendment III.

[5] U. S. Constitution, Amendment IV.

[6] U. S. Constitution, Amendment V.

the *Federal* Government was to be a government of express and limited powers, and that all rights and powers not delegated to it were retained by the people and the individual States. Until today no member of this Court has ever suggested that the Ninth Amendment meant anything else, and the idea that a federal court could ever use the Ninth Amendment to annul a law passed by the elected representatives of the people of the State of Connecticut would have caused James Madison no little wonder.

What provision of the Constitution, then, does make this state law invalid? The Court says it is the right of privacy "created by several fundamental constitutional guarantees." With all deference, I can find no such general right of privacy in the Bill of Rights, in any other part of the Constitution, or in any case ever before decided by this Court.[7]

At the oral argument in this case we were told that the Connecticut law does not "conform to current community standards." But it is not the function of this Court to decide cases on the basis of community standards. We are here to decide cases "agreeably to the Constitution and laws of the United States." It is the essence of judicial

---

[7] Cases like *Shelton* v. *Tucker*, 364 U. S. 479 and *Bates* v. *Little Rock*, 361 U. S. 516, relied upon in the concurring opinions today, dealt with true First Amendment rights of association and are wholly inapposite here. See also, *e. g.*, *NAACP* v. *Alabama*, 357 U. S. 449; *Edwards* v. *South Carolina*, 372 U. S. 229. Our decision in *McLaughlin* v. *Florida*, 379 U. S. 184, is equally far afield. That case held invalid under the Equal Protection Clause, a state criminal law which discriminated against Negroes.

The Court does not say how far the new constitutional right of privacy announced today extends. See, *e. g.*, Mueller, Legal Regulation of Sexual Conduct, at 127; Ploscowe, Sex and the Law, at 189. I suppose, however, that even after today a State can constitutionally still punish at least some offenses which are not committed in public.

duty to subordinate our own personal views, our own ideas of what legislation is wise and what is not.   If, as I should surely hope, the law before us does not reflect the standards of the people of Connecticut, the people of Connecticut can freely exercise their true Ninth and Tenth Amendment rights to persuade their elected representatives to repeal it.   That is the constitutional way to take this law off the books.[8]

---

[8] See *Reynolds* v. *Sims,* 377 U. S. 533, 562.   The Connecticut House of Representatives recently passed a bill (House Bill No. 2462) repealing the birth control law.   The State Senate has apparently not yet acted on the measure, and today is relieved of that responsibility by the Court.   New Haven Journal-Courier, Wed., May 19, 1965, p. 1, col. 4, and p. 13, col. 7.